THE MamaZen PARENTING Method

THE MamaZen PARENTING Method

7 STEPS TO STOP YELLING, CALM YOUR STRESS, AND RAISE CONFIDENT KIDS

IRIN RUBIN
FOUNDER OF THE AWARD-WINNING MAMAZEN APP

The MamaZen Parenting Method
© 2025 Irin Rubin

All rights reserved. No part of this publication may be reproduced, stored in a retrieval system, or transmitted in any form or by any means, electronic, mechanical, photocopying, recording, or otherwise, without prior permission from the author.

First edition published by Inner Path Press

Disclaimer:

This book is not intended to replace professional medical advice, diagnosis, or treatment. If you are experiencing severe anxiety, postpartum depression, or other mental health concerns, please consult a licensed healthcare provider.

To my husband, Jake

In the unpredictable world of parenthood, your love and support
have been the steady force I could always count on.
Thank you for giving me the space to grow—not only as a mother,
but as a leader with a mission to help other moms feel seen,
supported, and empowered.

To my daughters, Eden and Mia

You are my heart, my why, and the reason this work exists.
It is because of you, and for you, that I continue to grow.
Everything I've built began with the love I have for you.

To my parents, Eli and Miki

Thank you for all the sacrifices and the dedication it took to be supportive and
caring parents.
And for loving me to the moon and back,
every single day since I was born.

Contents

INTRO: The Missing Piece of Modern Parenting   ix

PART 1: The Awakening   1

1. You Are Not Broken   3
2. The Birth Plan That Never Happened   9
3. Postpartum PTSD Struck Again!   19
4. Medication Wasn't Going to Fix This   27
5. No Village, Just Me   33
6. Traditional Parenting Advice Was Useless   39
7. Calm-Quat: Why You Can't Hack Your Way to Calm   45

PART 2: The Shift Begins   55

8. When the Fog Began to Lift   57
9. The Ripple Effect of Dysregulation   67
10. Before You Snap   77

PART 3: Rewiring from the Inside Out   91

11. Rewiring Your Nervous System   93
12. The Wound Beneath the Trigger   107

13.	Setting Daily Intentions	125
14.	Rewrite the Script	135

PART 4: Deepening the Practice — 151

15.	Mindfulness Matters	153
16.	Parenting by Design, Not Default	167
17.	Mind Training for Moms	177

PART 5: Living the Transformation — 187

18.	The Power of Presence	189
19.	Co-Regulation: Calm Is Contagious	197
20.	Choosing Harmony Every Day	209

INTRODUCTION

The Missing Piece of Modern Parenting

It was 2 a.m. I woke up drenched in sweat—not from the heat, but from anxiety—jolted by my baby's cries. I prayed she wouldn't wake my toddler. My husband was still lost in dreamland, while I had to move fast. What did she need? She had eight pacifiers scattered around her crib—had she lost them all? My mind started racing. I didn't have a bottle ready. I silently begged her to fall back asleep easily.

I held her in my arms, second-guessing everything. Maybe I rushed in too quickly. Maybe now she'd expect to wake at this hour every night. *Shit,* I thought, *I don't know what I'm doing.* She calmed down a little, and I gently laid her back down, hoping against hope. I closed her door quietly ... and then the wailing started again. I sighed and opened the door. It was going to be another sleepless night. I hated 2 a.m. wake-ups. I needed her to sleep. I needed to sleep.

The next morning, I was a wreck, just like every other day. I chugged my coffee, knowing I'd need a few more to make it through. I was tired. I was unhappy. My toddler seemed cheerful—for now. My husband looked bright-eyed and refreshed, excited to head off to the office. I clung to a small hope that maybe today my baby would nap for more than twenty minutes. But deep down, I knew better.

When my husband casually asked how I slept, I felt invisible arrows of anger shoot from my eyes towards him. I forced a grin. "I think Mia is having another growth spurt," I muttered. Growth spurts—I hated them. They destroyed any shred of a sleep routine I'd managed to build. They seemed to come every week. My baby was almost a year old—I had survived about 30+ growth spurts by now.

The day dragged on. We played. We sang. We went for a stroller walk. I was tired through all of it, but I smiled for my baby anyway. Then came the afternoon chaos: dinner, baths, endless bedtime struggles. The hours stretched, testing my patience to its very last thread. Whining, clinging, not listening—and I felt myself slipping. I saw it happening, but I was too deep in. I hated how it felt, but I couldn't stop it. So, I snapped at everyone.

After bedtime, I went downstairs carrying a heavy blanket of guilt. My husband sat on the couch, distant and serious. He looked at me and said, "You know things need to change. If we're still like this a year from now, we're going to have to make some hard decisions."

His words were heavy. I felt scared. I felt lost. The truth is that I didn't even recognize myself anymore. But somewhere deep inside, a small voice whispered: *You can do this. You can break this cycle.*

For years, I thought the problem was the kids. If they only stopped waking me up at night. If they would just listen. If they would whine and fight less. If they could be easier, better—maybe I could finally be the mother I wanted to be. The patient one. The calm one. A version of me I could actually be proud of. Like the glowing, beatific mothers who floated across my Instagram and TikTok feeds and seemed to have it all figured out.

Or maybe—I told myself—if I could just find the perfect parenting technique. A better strategy. A tighter schedule. Some magical system to manage the chaos. Then maybe I could fix the brokenness that was seeping out of me and spreading into our whole family.

But I had it backward.

Parenting isn't just about how we respond to our children. It's about how we tend to ourselves.

That night was one of many that broke me open. But over time, I began to learn something no parenting book had ever taught me: the real work wasn't fixing my kids—it was healing myself. The more I focused on calming my own storms, the more everything began to shift.

I began sharing what I was learning—first with friends, then with other mothers, and eventually through my work with MamaZen.

For years, I poured everything I had into helping other moms find the path I had struggled to discover on my own.

And then one day, a message landed in my inbox—one of hundreds over the years—and something about it struck deeper. It wasn't the first time a mother had poured out her guilt, her regret, her hope. But this one made something crystal clear: it was time to put this method into words. To shape it. Name it. Share it.

This mom shared the following in her email:

> *This morning, I told myself I'd be patient. I really meant it. But then my 8-year-old started yelling at me for nothing. Then he cussed. And instead of staying calm, I cussed right back, louder, meaner. I lost it. Again.*
> *When I dropped him off at school, I told him I loved him, but honestly? I felt relieved he wasn't my problem for a few hours. And then I got home, and the guilt hit. Hard.*
> *I grabbed my phone and started scrolling, looking for answers. Parenting tips, behavior hacks, TikTok videos—anything that could help me figure out why he's behaving this way. And then I found MamaZen, and realized, it's me. I'm the one who needs to change.*
> *I can't keep meeting his chaos with my own.*
>
> *Thank you for creating this. For the first time in a long time, I have hope.*

Her words echoed what I had once lived. And they reminded me why this work matters so deeply. Because when a mother begins to heal, everything around her begins to change.

You can walk into any bookstore or scroll through Amazon and find thousands of parenting books—schedules, sleep training methods, discipline hacks. Tens of thousands of tips and tricks, all promising to make it easier. We are drowning in advice.

And yet, here we are. Still exhausted. Still overwhelmed. Still waking up every morning wondering, *"Why does it feel like I'm the only one who can't figure this out?"*

Because it was never just about finding the right strategy. It's about healing the storm inside. And no one ever taught us how to do that.

The MamaZen Method was born out of that need.

At first, it wasn't a method—it was survival.
It began as a way for me to heal myself.
To find a steadier, calmer way to meet the daily demands of motherhood without losing my mind, my center, or my soul.

Slowly, it grew into something more.
Something bigger than just me.

It became a path that has helped countless mothers reconnect to themselves, repair their relationships with their children, bring more peace into their homes, and rediscover joy—real joy—in motherhood.

In 2020, I launched the MamaZen app to put a radically different approach to parenting into the hands of parents around the world. Since then, MamaZen has been trusted by over half a million mothers across more than 30 countries, and was honored with the prestigious EDC Innovation Award for its impact in maternal mental health.

This book is the next step in that journey. An extension of the MamaZen universe—and an invitation for you to step inside.

Throughout its pages you will find real stories from mothers just like you (including many from the frontline of my own mothering battlefield) as well as an introduction to the MamaZen Method, a process born from my own pain and struggle, and one that has already helped thousands of real mothers like you rebuild their emotional foundation from the inside out.

I know that when you're overwhelmed, hurting, and exhausted, change like this can feel too big, too far away, too hard to reach. That's why I've broken The Method into 7 simple, powerful steps. Even on the hardest of days these steps can be a lifeline and when practiced consistently, they carry you somewhere entirely new.

You'll start by reconnecting to yourself—to the steady center that often gets lost in the swirl of the commotion of domestic life.
You'll learn how to meet frustration without losing yourself.
How to soften the voice of guilt.
How to step out of old cycles of yelling and regret.
How to forgive yourself for the days you stumble, and how to build the strength to rise again.

Each step builds on the last, creating a new foundation inside you: calm, resilient, and deeply rooted. The 7 Steps aren't about controlling your child's behavior or learning a new parenting technique. They're about rewiring your inner world, so you can meet whatever chaos comes your way with steadiness, clarity, and connection.

Through this process, you won't just change the way you parent. You'll change the way you live.

How to Use This Book

This book is meant to be read in order—step by step, chapter by chapter. Each section builds on the one before it, guiding you through a transformational journey with intention and care.

- **Chapters 1–7** lay the groundwork. They reveal why change is necessary and help you understand the deeper patterns shaping your experience.

- **Chapters 8–17** walk you through each of the **7 Steps of the MamaZen Method**, giving you the tools and insights to shift how you think, feel, and show up as a parent.

- **Chapters 18–20** help you integrate everything you've learned—so it becomes a living, breathing part of your everyday life.

You'll also find a **Quick Reference Guide to the 7 Steps** on page 217, which you can return to anytime for clarity and encouragement.

At the end of each chapter, you'll find a **MamaZen Moment**—a simple, grounding practice to help you pause, reflect, and realign with the parent and person you want to be.

Think of this book as your steady guide—a hand on your back reminding you: You are not alone. You are not broken. And real, lasting change is possible.

By the time you finish, you won't just know how to stay calm, you'll feel the shift in your bones.

You'll stop living in fear of the next tantrum or meltdown.
You'll love your life more.
You'll love yourself more. And that love will ripple outward, touching your children in ways you can't even imagine yet.

If you're ready to stop surviving and start living, if you're ready to come home to yourself, you're in the right place.

Let's begin!

PART 1
The Awakening

CHAPTER 1

You Are Not Broken

"I am not crazy!" I kept telling myself, but my mind wouldn't stop racing.
What happened to me?
Why do I feel this way?
I should be happy. I should be grateful for having two healthy kids. So why did I feel like the only place I could find peace was under a rock in the woods?

I used to joke about inventing a sleepaway camp for moms—a place where we could finally rest and recharge without the weight of the world pressing down on us. But deep down, it wasn't just a joke. The feeling of wanting to escape my parenting life was so present, so real, and so overwhelming.

I loved my kids more than anything, but that love didn't erase the exhaustion, the anxiety, or the relentless mental load. I kept thinking: *Am I missing something? Am I just not cut out for this?* Because this—this drained, irritable, on-edge version of me—was not the mother I thought I would be.

Before I had kids, I thought I was ready. I read all the "101" parenting books. I made the perfect birth plan. We went to parenting classes. I had visions of rocking my baby in a peaceful nursery, humming lullabies, soaking in the magic of motherhood. I imagined mornings filled with giggles, afternoons playing in the sunshine, and nights cuddling up for bedtime stories.

But no one told me about the *other* side of motherhood.

No one told me about the sleepless nights that bleed into foggy, endless days. No one told me that breastfeeding might feel like a battle—or that my body wouldn't feel like my own anymore. No one told me that the exhaustion wouldn't just be physical—it would be emotional, mental, and so deep in my bones that no amount of coffee could touch it.

And no one warned me I'd have moments where I would feel like disappearing. Where I'd hide in the bathroom just to steal a moment of silence. Where I'd sit in the car for an extra five minutes before walking into the chaos again.

Where was *this* version of motherhood in the books? Why did it look so effortless in movies? Where were the moms crying quietly in the kitchen, wondering if they had anything left to give?

Because that was the version of motherhood I was living. And for a long time, I thought I was the only one.

Somewhere along the way, society decided that good mothers don't complain. We're supposed to love every second. We're supposed to feel nothing but gratitude. We're supposed to enjoy motherhood like it's a dream come true, every single day.

But here's the truth: Motherhood is exhausting. Not just physically—but mentally and emotionally. We are stretched too thin. The days feel like a marathon, and yet nothing ever feels "done." The pressure never stops. The constant worrying, the decision fatigue, the invisible workload—it's relentless.

> *You were never meant to carry it all on your own.*

We are always needed, but rarely replenished. We give and give until there's nothing left … and then we feel guilty for wanting a break.

So we don't say it out loud. We smile. We push through. We do what we have to do. Because that's what moms do, right?

But between sleepless nights and endless responsibilities, I lost something. Not just time. Not just energy. I lost my mind.

I became the emotional backbone for everyone—my kids, my husband, my family, even my dog. I absorbed their stress, their worries, their needs. But who was absorbing mine?

I wasn't just tired—I was emotionally and mentally depleted. I didn't have time to process my own feelings because I was too busy managing everyone else's.

This is what I now understand to be **emotional burnout**—the slow, silent draining of a mother's inner reserves. It's also called **invisible labor**—the work no one sees but that we carry in our minds, our bodies, and our hearts every single day.

And the hardest part? We start to believe that this is just how motherhood feels. That we're supposed to feel this overwhelmed. That it's normal to feel like we're barely hanging on.

But what if it's not? What if we were never meant to carry this much, this alone?

This is why the MamaZen Method exists—not to give you more to do, but to finally help you carry *less*. It's not about parenting harder. It's about parenting from a place of calm, clarity, and connection—starting with you.

If you've ever thought, *I just need a break*, or *Why does this feel so much harder than I expected?*—I want you to know something:

It was never just you.
You are not broken.
You are not failing.
You are not crazy.
You are human.

> **6 Signs You're Carrying Too Much Emotional Weight**
>
> ▸ You snap at small things, even when you don't want to
>
> ▸ Your sleep is broken—or you lie awake despite being exhausted
>
> ▸ You feel guilty, no matter how much you do
>
> ▸ Your mind feels foggy or scattered
>
> ▸ Your inner voice is more critical than kind
>
> ▸ You wake up feeling emotionally drained before the day begins
>
> *If you see yourself here, you're not failing—you're overloaded.*

And motherhood—while beautiful—is one of the hardest things a person can do.

This book won't give you more advice to fix your kids. Instead, it will guide you to fix the way you *feel* in motherhood. So you're not just surviving it—but actually *living* it.

Because something has to change.
And that change starts now.

The first step?
Reconnecting to *yourself*—and building a foundation strong enough to hold *you*, not just everyone else.

> **MamaZen Moment**
>
> *You Are Not Broken*
>
> **Reflection:**
> Close your eyes for a moment.
> Feel the weight you've been carrying.
> Whisper to yourself: *I am not broken. I am human.*
>
> **Reframe:**
> *Motherhood isn't hard because I'm doing it wrong.*
> *It's hard because it asks everything of me—*
> *and I was never meant to carry it all alone.*
>
> **Practice:**
> *Place your hand over your heart.*
> *Breathe in slowly.*
> *And with the exhale, let go of just one drop of guilt.*

Amy's Story

For months, Amy believed she just wasn't cut out for motherhood. She was overwhelmed, anxious, and constantly on edge—and she blamed herself for not enjoying the moments everyone said she should cherish. It wasn't until she learned about emotional burnout and the invisible load that she realized: it wasn't her. **She wasn't broken—she was carrying too much, too silently, for too long.**

CHAPTER 2

The Birth Plan That Never Happened

We were so in love and so excited to be pregnant. Becoming parents was a childhood dream for both of us—something we had imagined for years.

We were ready.

We took classes, followed all the advice, and prepared for everything. The hospital bag was packed weeks in advance. I had memorized every breathing technique from my hypnobirthing lessons.

I had the perfect birth plan.
We were going to do this right.

My husband even had his own checklist. "You should breastfeed for at least two years," he told me one day, convinced we were going to be the ultimate natural, attachment-style parents.

"Sure!" I said with full confidence.

Looking back now, I was so delusional.

Pregnancy was fun—until it wasn't.

Everything was going smoothly, and then, just a few weeks before my due date, we went in for a routine ultrasound. We expected to see our healthy baby, to smile, and feel reassured that everything was still on track.

Instead, the doctor's face changed.

He frowned at the screen. He measured something. Then he measured it again.

"Your baby has IUGR (Intrauterine Growth Restriction)," he said.

I stared at him. I didn't even know what that meant.

"What do we do?" I asked, my stomach tightening with fear.

He barely hesitated. "Pick a date this week. We're inducing you."

Induce me?!

I had a perfect birth plan! I was going to go into labor naturally, experience everything the way my body was meant to. I had spent months preparing for an unmedicated, beautiful, calm birth.

None of that mattered now.

My body wasn't in control anymore. The doctor had decided for me.

I was terrified.
I started crying.
The doctor sighed.

"You can cry, but that's not going to help anything," he said, completely void of emotion.

Talk about bedside manner.

I felt like my world had just collapsed.
Everything I had planned for, everything I thought I could control, was gone in an instant.

I knew labor contractions were supposed to start gradually, building up over time, giving my body space to adjust.
That's not what happened.

> **When Your Birth Plan Changes**
>
> ▸ Grieve the plan you imagined
> ▸ Anchor yourself in the present moment
> ▸ Remember: *You have not failed*

Because I was induced, my body was forced into labor before it was ready. The contractions hit fast and hard—one after another, with barely any break in between. It was relentless.
Neither my baby nor I had time to adjust to the intensity.

I remember gripping the hospital bed, gasping for air, trying to find any relief, but there was none.
My body wasn't prepared. My baby wasn't prepared.
The stress was overwhelming.

And then came the pain.
I thought I had prepared for labor pains. I thought I knew what to expect.

But nothing—nothing—prepared me for this.

Every time the nurse checked me, it felt like the most excruciating pain—like I was being punched from the inside.
I gritted my teeth and tried to breathe through it, but nothing prepared me for that kind of pain.

Then, they popped my water manually.
The shock, the discomfort, the sudden intensity—I could barely process it.

My body wasn't doing what it was supposed to on its own, so they were forcing it.

Then came the fever.
I felt hot and weak. My body ached. I was shivering for hours. I could barely keep my eyes open.
The exhaustion felt impossible.

And then I heard the words no mother ever wants to hear: "You have an infection."

I wanted to scream, but I didn't even have the energy for that.

I felt like I had been hit by a truck, but shhh—don't tell anyone.
Because new moms aren't supposed to complain.
We're supposed to be strong.

It took me 23 hours and 15 minutes to deliver my beautiful baby. And I remembered every moment of it.

The delivery room was filled with nurses, NICU staff, doctors—it felt like a full room.
As soon as she arrived, she was taken to the NICU section in the delivery room.

I was left alone with my doctor.
My husband, my mother, and every staff member—everyone was surrounding my baby.
I lay there, silent, exhausted, invisible.

And that is how I felt from that moment on.

Then the pediatrician broke the news:
We had to stay in the hospital for ten days.
Ten. Days.

My baby was put on two antibiotics and had to be taken for treatment twice a day.

While other moms were taking their newborns home, I was stuck in a hospital bed—overwhelmed, in pain, and emotionally shattered.

I wanted to breastfeed, but the stress, exhaustion, and antibiotic schedule completely disrupted our feeding routine.

I felt like a failure before I even got to take my baby home.

When we finally got to go home, I looked at my husband and said, "Are they just going to let us take her home?"

I had no idea how I was supposed to take care of this tiny human. I was terrified.

Nothing felt natural.
Her relentless screams sent waves of anxiety through me.
Desperate for answers, I turned to the internet and discovered she had colic.

> *This isn't how I imagined it. But it doesn't mean I've done anything wrong.*

I had heard of colic before, but I never realized how much anxiety it could trigger in a new mom.

For the next three months, like clockwork, she screamed from 4 to 7 p.m. every single night.

Nothing helped.
I was exhausted beyond words.

The stress, the trauma from the hospital, the screaming—it all felt like too much.

I had postpartum PTSD.
Motherhood didn't start with soft lullabies and snuggles for me.
It started with fear, pain, and exhaustion.

For months, I struggled to process what had happened.

4 Signs of Emotional Overload in Postpartum

- You feel invisible, even when people are around
- You cry easily—sometimes without knowing why
- Small things trigger big waves of anxiety
- You feel like you're failing, even when you're trying your best

I had spent my whole life believing that if I planned enough, worked hard enough, and did everything the right way, I would get the outcome I wanted.

But motherhood doesn't work like that.
It doesn't reward perfection or planning.
It humbles you. It strips you down.
And when you're left raw and rattled, you realize—there's no going back to who you were before.

It took me a long time to admit how much I was struggling.
Longer to ask for help.
Even longer to understand that I wasn't broken—I was overwhelmed. Traumatized. Drowning.

The only thing I could actually control was how I reacted to the chaos.
Because if I had learned earlier how to manage my mind instead of trying to control everything else, I would have suffered so much less.

I couldn't see it at the time—I was completely consumed by the chaos.
I didn't have a method. I didn't have awareness.
What I had was pain.
And sometimes, that's where the real story begins—not with clarity, but with collapse.

And then, somewhere deep in the fog, a quiet thought surfaced:
There has to be another way.

That thought was the beginning of a long road to awareness—one with ups and downs, setbacks, and small wins.
It didn't change everything overnight. But it cracked something open.

In this book, I'll help you get to that *aha* moment faster—without needing to fall apart first.
Because awareness doesn't have to begin at rock bottom.
It can start right here, right now—with you choosing to see things differently.

This is where Step 1 of the MamaZen Method begins:
Learning how to reconnect to yourself—gently, bravely, one feeling at a time. (See the *7 Step Quick Reference Guide* at the back of the book.)

MamaZen Moment

Softening Around the Chaos

Reflection:
Think back to a moment when the ground shifted under you.
Place your hand over your heart and whisper:
It's safe to not have all the answers.
It's safe to be carried sometimes.

Reframe:
True strength isn't about controlling everything.
It's about trusting yourself to meet whatever arises.

Practice:

When something feels overwhelming today:

Pause.

Take one full breath.

Say to yourself: *I give myself permission to soften.*

Jasmine's Story

Jasmine spent months preparing for an unmedicated birth. But when her labor stalled and her baby's heart rate dropped, everything changed—fast. She was rushed into surgery, shaking and terrified, completely unprepared for the cold, clinical reality of a c-section. For a long time, she felt like her first moment of motherhood had been taken from her. But, in time, she realized: how her baby entered the world didn't define her—**what mattered was how she moved forward, with love—for herself and her baby.**

CHAPTER 3

Postpartum PTSD Struck Again!

My second delivery was easier.

There was no traumatic induction, no fever, no ten-day hospital stay. This time, I had a better idea of what to expect, and everything seemed … better this time around.

Until it wasn't.

Because my second baby had a severe colic. Not the *"fussy in the evening"* kind of colic—the *screaming-for-eight-hours-a-day* kind.

And she would nap for only 20-30 minutes max.

I felt like I was losing my mind again. It was wintertime, and her cries were bouncing off the walls.

I had survived my first baby's colic and thought nothing could be worse.

But when I found myself trapped in the same cycle again—this time with a toddler to care for too—the overwhelm broke me.

Every scream, every hour of inconsolable crying, felt like a direct attack on my nervous system.

It was like I was reliving the trauma of my first postpartum experience, only this time, I wasn't just caring for a colicky baby.

I was managing two kids, and I had nothing left in me.

I would hold my baby, rocking, bouncing, trying everything—gas drops, swaddling, changing my diet, cutting dairy, Baby Bjorn—nothing worked.

And the worst part?

Everyone kept telling me, *"You're a second-time mom, you know what you're doing now."*

But I didn't feel like I knew what I was doing at all.

I flipped through my hospital packet, desperately looking for something—anything—that could help me alleviate my stress.

A guide for overwhelmed moms. A page titled *"What to Do When You Feel Like You're Drowning."*

Some kind of reassurance that what I was feeling was normal—and that there was a way through it.

But there was nothing.

It was 2016, and in all those neatly printed pages, there wasn't a single resource to help a mother find relief.

At my six-week postpartum checkup, I finally brought up how I was feeling.

The exhaustion. The stress. The feeling that I was constantly on edge.

I wasn't sleeping enough. I wasn't eating a balanced diet. My body felt like it was constantly bracing for the next scream, the next sleepless night, the next moment of feeling like I was failing.

My doctor shrugged his shoulders and said, *"Everything seems fine. You can go back to normal life now."*

Fine.

Normal?!

Nothing felt fine or normal.

But because my PPD questionnaire wasn't alarming, my doctor shrugged his shoulders, and off I went.

I had just told them that I was drowning. That I didn't feel like myself. That I was exhausted, depleted, and emotionally drained.

But because I didn't have the identifiable symptoms of PPD, the doctor didn't think I needed anything else, or maybe he just didn't have anything else to give me. I was sent away to my "normal" new reality.

Like so many moms are.

We hear a lot about postpartum depression (PPD)—and we should. One in seven moms experience it.

But what about the other six?

The ones who don't fit the "clinical diagnosis." The ones who aren't *fine*—but aren't "bad enough" to get help.

Where do they get help?

What happens to the moms who are barely holding it together but are told, *"This is just motherhood. You'll adjust."*

We talk about the 1 in 7 who are diagnosed.
But in reality, all mothers ride the emotional rollercoaster of new motherhood.

And just because you don't have PPD doesn't mean you're okay.

We call it the "baby blues," and it "usually" fades within 6 to 8 weeks.

But what happens when the baby blues don't go away? What if they linger for months—or even a year?

What if the exhaustion, the overwhelm, the emotional weight never lifts?

At what point does it stop being *just* the baby blues? And why does no one talk about it?

That's what my life had become—a constant state of survival.

Surviving the sleepless nights.
Surviving the stress.
Surviving the guilt that I wasn't doing enough for my kids.
Surviving the anxiety that I was failing all of us.

I was barely surviving.

But is that really what motherhood is supposed to feel like?

We are expected to just figure it out, move on, and function as if we're fine.

But I wasn't fine.

And neither are so many other moms who are dismissed just because they don't fit into a diagnosis.

One night, after another brutal day of crying, bouncing, screaming, rocking, guilt, and exhaustion, I sat in the dark with my baby, feeling numb.

I didn't feel like me anymore.

And that's when I knew—I couldn't keep doing this.

> **5 Signs You're Stuck in Survival Mode**
>
> - Constantly bracing for the next meltdown
> - Emotional outbursts— crying, yelling, shutting down
> - Guilt hits hard afterward
> - Disconnected from joy, yourself, or your kids
> - A quiet belief: *I'm failing at this*
>
> *Survival mode isn't failure. It's your nervous system trying to keep you safe.*

I couldn't keep going through the motions, pretending I was fine, waiting for things to magically get better.

Because motherhood wasn't going to get easier. I had to change the way I experienced it.

I didn't have the words for it back then, but that night in the dark was the first tiny crack where something new began to break through.

A shift.
A whisper.
The beginning of something I now understand as the **first and most important step of transformation.**

Step 1 of the MamaZen Method: Awareness.

Awareness doesn't mean having it all figured out. It means finally seeing the truth of where you are.
That you're not okay. That you need something to change.
It's the moment you stop pushing it down—and start facing it with compassion.

That night, I didn't suddenly have answers. I didn't know what to do next. But I had seen the truth: *I wasn't fine.* And that single moment of honesty was so important; that's how my healing began.

> **This is not the end of the story. This is the moment something shifts.**

Because you can't change what you can't see.
And once you *see it*—you can begin to shift it.

MamaZen Moment

This Is the Moment Change Begins

Reflection:
Think of a moment when you knew something had to change— when surviving wasn't enough anymore.
Breathe in.
Breathe out.
Whisper to yourself: *This is not the end of the story. This is the beginning.*

Reframe:
Reaching a breaking point isn't a failure.
It's a doorway.

Practice:
Place one hand on your heart, one on your belly.
Feel both rise and fall.
Remind yourself: *Even now, there is a way forward.*

Elena's Story

Elena sat in her parked car, hands shaking, afraid to walk back inside. Her newborn had screamed for hours, her toddler had melted down twice, and she hadn't eaten all day. The kids were finally inside with their dad—but she couldn't do it, not yet. She kept telling herself to just breathe, to just push through like she always did—but something in her broke. That day, she whispered, *I can't do this anymore.* And while nothing changed right then, something opened: the truth. **She wasn't fine—and finally admitting it became the first step toward finding her way back.**

CHAPTER 4

Medication Wasn't Going to Fix This

I had tried *everything* to feel better—changing my diet, taking supplements, even taking medication my doctor shouldn't have prescribed. I had spent months searching for relief, grasping at anything that might help.

After going to numerous doctor appointments and running lab tests, which all came back normal, my doctor decided to put me on thyroid medication to help with my exhaustion. I trusted his recommendation—after all, I was desperate for relief.

Every morning, I would still wake up exhausted. The kind of exhaustion that seeps into your bones, that no amount of sleep can fix. I waited for the medication to help, but nothing changed. I still felt like I was dragging myself through quicksand every single day.

Frustrated, a few months later I decided to see a thyroid specialist. Within minutes, she looked at my case and said, "You're not supposed to be on this medication. Let's get you off of it before it messes up your thyroid function."

It was a wake-up call.

Instead of addressing the root cause—the stress, the overwhelm, the unrealistic expectations placed on mothers—I was given a prescription.

Because that's the default.

When mothers say they are exhausted, anxious, or overwhelmed, they are told they need medication.

Feeling burned out? *Here's an antidepressant.*
Struggling with patience? *Maybe you need anxiety meds.*
Can't focus because your brain is overloaded with a thousand tiny details? *Have you considered ADHD medication?*

And while medication can be a helpful tool for some, it is not a replacement for real solutions. It does not replace rest, support, community, or systemic change. It does not fix the fact that mothers are overworked, undervalued, and often left to carry the impossible burden of doing everything alone.

There is a weight that many carry, yet few recognize. It is not written on to-do lists, nor is it neatly checked off at the end of the day. It lingers in the background of every moment, shaping decisions, dictating emotions, and filling the spaces between tasks.

It is the invisible mental load, the unseen burden that so many, especially mothers, bear in silence.

It begins in the early hours of the morning, long before the household stirs. The mental checklist starts ticking before feet even hit the floor—what needs to be packed for school? Is there milk for breakfast? Did the permission slip get signed? And as the day unfolds, this list only grows: keeping track of appointments, remembering birthdays, anticipating emotional needs, and solving problems before they even arise. It's the countless things no one else thinks about but always seem to get done.

This load is not just about logistics—it is deeply emotional. It is the mental effort of remembering who likes their sandwich cut into triangles and who prefers squares. It is sensing the shift in a child's mood and knowing they need extra reassurance. It is anticipating a spouse's stress level and adjusting your own responses accordingly. It is being the keeper of everything, the invisible safety net, the quiet force making sure nothing unravels.

Yet, despite its constant presence, the mental load is rarely acknowledged. It is invisible because it is expected. When things run smoothly, no one notices the effort behind it. But when something is forgotten—when the birthday card is missing, when the clean clothes run out, when a deadline is missed—it is suddenly visible, often met with frustration or blame.

This weight is exhausting. It leads to burnout, resentment, and the quiet erosion of self.
It is why so many mothers feel overwhelmed even when they appear to have everything "under control."

The world sees only what is done, not the mental effort it takes to keep everything in motion.

The medication didn't fix everything. It didn't erase the exhaustion, the anger, the guilt.
But it did challenge me to think:
What if I could meet these moments differently?

> **It's safe to imagine a better way.**

That thought didn't give me the answer. But it opened the door.

That's the heart of Step 1 in the MamaZen Method: Awareness.
Noticing what's really happening—not just around you, but inside you.
The expectations you carry.
The patterns you've been stuck in.
The belief that it's all on you.

Awareness doesn't always feel like an epiphany. Sometimes, it starts with frustration. Sometimes, it's a quiet *"I can't live like this anymore."*
But once you begin to see the truth of where you are—
you finally have the power to change it.

What "Awareness" Looks Like

- *Noticing you're about to spiral*
- *Naming the feeling: I'm overwhelmed. I'm terrified. I'm angry.*
- *Letting go of judgment*
- *Remembering: This moment doesn't define me.*

Catching yourself isn't weakness—it's the beginning of strength.

MamaZen Moment

Cracking Open to Something New

Reflection:
Think back to a moment when surviving wasn't enough—
when you knew you wanted to start living again.
Breathe in deeply.
As you exhale, whisper: *It's safe to imagine a better way.*

Reframe:
The smallest cracks are how the light gets in.

Practice:
When you feel yourself starting to spiral today,
place one hand on your heart, one on your belly.
Inhale and say: *I am allowed to slow down.*
Exhale and say: *I am allowed to find a new way.*

Jessica's Story

Jessica struggled with anxiety, and her first instinct was to try to control everyone and everything around her. But when that failed—as it always did—she felt even more helpless. Some days, she hit her lowest point and had no one left to vent to. Therapy appointments took too long to get, and she didn't want to rely on medication alone.

"What finally helped was using this method. It brought me back to center—and suddenly, I felt okay again. My patience returned. My peace returned. And so did my hope."
—*Jessica, MamaZen Member*

CHAPTER 5

No Village, Just Me

There was a time when raising a child was not a solitary act. Mothers were surrounded by grandmothers, sisters, neighbors, and friends—a village of hands to rock the baby, to prepare meals, to reassure a weary mother that she was not alone. There was wisdom passed down, shoulders to lean on, a shared understanding that parenting was never meant to be done in isolation.

But those villages have vanished—and while we've all heard that before, the weight of their absence is still deeply felt.

Modern life has scattered families across states and countries. Communities have thinned, replaced by digital connections that do little to fill the void of real human support. The neighbor who once dropped by unannounced to offer a helping hand now stays behind closed doors. The extended family who once lived under one roof now connects through occasional phone calls and holiday visits. The elders who once guided young mothers through the trenches of early parenthood are now absent, their wisdom drowned out by an overwhelming sea of conflicting advice found online.

And what did we replace these villages with?

Absolutely, nothing.

Instead, we handed mothers an impossible burden and told them to carry it alone. We romanticized the idea of the "supermom" who does it all without breaking, without needing help, without ever saying, "I can't do this alone." We glorified self-sufficiency to the point that asking for support now feels like failure.

We replaced villages with isolation. With mothers pacing in nurseries at midnight—exhausted, overstimulated, and with no one to pass the baby to. With women drowning in postpartum anxiety, scrolling through social media looking for connection, only to find curated perfection that deepens their loneliness. With parents questioning every decision, wishing there was someone to turn to, but feeling like they should have all the answers on their own.

> You don't have to be perfect to be exactly what your child needs.

And yet, we wonder why so many mothers are struggling.

It wasn't supposed to be like this. Parenting was never meant to be a solo journey.

The weight of raising a child, of shaping a life, was always meant to be shared. We were meant to lean on each other, to step in when one of us was struggling, to hold the crying baby while the mother slept, to remind each other that we are not alone in this.

That's why the MamaZen Method doesn't ask you to be perfect.

It teaches you how to work with what's real: your feelings, your triggers, your energy, right where you are. Calm, connection, and confidence don't come from chasing perfection. They come from learning how to catch yourself and to reset when it's messy.

> **Are You Caught in the Myth of the Perfect Mom**
>
> ▸ Constantly comparing yourself to other moms (especially online)
> ▸ Feeling guilty no matter how much you do
> ▸ Believing *"good moms don't get angry, sad, or tired"*
> ▸ Measuring your worth by how much you get done
>
> *The perfect mom doesn't exist. But the present one does—and she's enough.*

MamaZen Moment

Presence Over Perfection

Reflection:
Think of one image of the "perfect mom" you've carried in your mind.
Now, gently imagine letting it dissolve—
like sand slipping through your fingers.

Reframe:
Your child doesn't need a perfect mom.
They need a human one—
willing to keep showing up with love.

Practice:
Every time you catch yourself chasing perfection today,
Pause.
Place a hand over your heart.
Whisper: *Presence, not perfection.*

Cecelia's Story

Cecelia had two kids under two, a husband who worked nights, and no family nearby. She was overwhelmed, exhausted, and convinced she had to do it all on her own. One day, during nap time, she finally paused—and chose herself instead of the dishes.

> **"I use this method whenever my kids are napping, and I'm able to reset myself. I'm always happy when they wake up."**
> —*Cecelia, MamaZen Member*

In that quiet moment, everything shifted. She realized her kids didn't need a perfect mom with a finished checklist—they just needed *her*—rested, grounded, and present.

CHAPTER 6

Traditional Parenting Advice Was Useless

Parenting books, online articles, well-meaning relatives—everyone has an opinion on how to raise kids. From sticker charts to time-outs, from "gentle parenting" to "tough love," there's no shortage of techniques promising to make children behave better, listen more, and stop pushing our buttons. And yet, here we are—more overwhelmed, more exhausted, and still wondering why nothing seems to work.

Most parenting advice assumes that if you just follow the right steps, your child will magically respond. But what happens when they don't? When time-outs don't curb tantrums, when praise doesn't build confidence, when your toddler still refuses to put on their shoes even after you've given them "two great choices"?

You start questioning yourself. Maybe you're not consistent enough. Maybe you need to be firmer. Maybe you need to be gentler. Maybe you're doing it all wrong.

And that's where the guilt and shame creep in.

Especially when you're out in public or around family.

Everyone stares at you and your child, silently wondering: Does she even know what she's doing? Her kid is *totally* playing her.

She should be more assertive.
She needs to discipline more.
Look, her child is having another meltdown.
Why is she feeding them that?!

The judgment is loud—even when no one says a word.

Because what's rarely acknowledged in all this criticism is how you feel. No one tells you that even the best discipline technique in the world won't work if you're running on empty. No one tells you that your child's behavior isn't a reflection of your worth as a parent. No one tells you that most of the chaos, the frustration, the exhaustion—isn't about your child at all.

> **Sometimes hitting the wall is the beginning of building a new one—only this time, it has a door.**

The real issue isn't whether you should use time-outs or time-ins. It's not whether positive reinforcement is better than consequences. It's not about any specific rule or method.

The real issue isn't about your discipline beliefs—it's about how we, as parents, feel inside. Our stress, exhaustion, and emotions shape our reactions, and our children respond to that.

Your child's behavior is a mirror. It reflects your stress, your exhaustion, your emotions. They don't need another parenting strategy; they need a parent who can show up for them with a calm, regulated presence. And that's the part that traditional parenting advice completely ignores.

Because here's the hard truth: You can't teach emotional regulation to a child while you're dysregulated yourself.

It doesn't matter how many deep breaths you tell them to take if you're snapping at them in frustration when they are having a meltdown. It doesn't matter how many times you tell them to use their words if you're overwhelmed and short-tempered.

> **4 Major Signs You're Near Emotional Collapse**
>
> ▶ Emotional numbness
> ▶ Explosive irritability over small things
> ▶ Exhaustion no amount of sleep can fix
> ▶ Feeling invisible, hopeless, or completely overwhelmed
>
> *Collapse doesn't mean you've failed. It means something needs to change.*

Children don't learn by being told. They learn by watching, by feeling, by experiencing the energy we bring into our home.

So instead of focusing on fixing their behavior, the real transformation begins when you start focusing on your own.

Instead of trying to control your child's behavior, you start learning how to regulate your own emotions.

Instead of trying to get them to listen, you start noticing how you communicate.

Instead of feeling frustrated that they aren't cooperating, you start understanding how your reactions are shaped by your own upbringing, stress, and subconscious patterns.

The more you change, the more their behavior shifts.

Not because you suddenly found the perfect parenting hack—but because your energy, your presence, and your mindset have changed.

And that's what makes The MamaZen Method different, yet so effective, it **begins here: the moment you stop blaming yourself—or your child—and start noticing the patterns you're stuck in. That's the moment you begin to wake up.**

MamaZen Moment

Your Rock Bottom Is Your Foundation

Reflection:
Think of a time when you felt like you couldn't go any further.
What did that moment ask of you?
What did it awaken in you?

Reframe:
Collapse isn't failure.
It's the call to rise—differently.

Practice:

When you feel overwhelmed today,

place a hand over your heart.

Whisper: *This is not the end.*

This is the beginning of something better.

Kat's Story

Kat was determined to parent differently. She had grown up with yelling, rigid rules, and emotional disconnection—and swore her kids would never feel what she felt. But when motherhood pushed her to the edge, all her good intentions crumbled. Despite reading the books, following the accounts, and trying every trick in the toolbox, her reactions told a different story.

"I wanted to be calm, but I kept snapping. I hated the mom I was becoming—and I felt powerless to stop it. MamaZen wasn't another tip to fix my kids. It helped me calm *me*. That's what I needed."
—*Kat, MamaZen Member*

With every Mindpower Session on the app, her nervous system settled. Her thoughts softened. And her connection with her children deepened.

Kat didn't need more advice—she needed a way to reconnect with herself. The shift didn't come from doing more. It came from finally learning how to feel calm, steady, and safe within.

CHAPTER 7

Calm-Quat: Why You Can't Hack Your Way to Calm

Bedtime took forever, again.

No one listened.

It was loud, chaotic, and overstimulating.

I could feel the tension rising in my body—a slow, creeping heat building behind my eyes and in the pit of my stomach. My patience was slipping, and I knew it. I didn't want to lose my cool, but the exhaustion had a grip on me, tightening with every second that dragged on.

"Get in bed."

No one moved.

"Come on. It's late."

Still, they kept talking, playing, jumping around like I hadn't spoken at all.

My voice sharpened. "I said get in bed!"

They whined, giggled, stalled.

Something inside me snapped.

I snapped at one of them, short, harsh, not even sure what I had said—only that my tone had turned sharp and biting.

Then I snapped again.

And again.

I walked fast, waved my hands, pointed to their beds, and made it clear I was done. The words came out clipped, too loud, too forceful.

I knew it wasn't their fault. They were just being kids. But I couldn't take it anymore.

It wasn't different from any other bedtime.

And yet, somehow, this time it felt worse.

My behavior was disgusting.

I hated how it felt.

I hated how I sounded.

But I couldn't seem to stop.

And then I heard it—

"Kumquat."

My husband's voice cut through the noise.

I knew what it meant.

But it didn't matter.

I was already too far gone, too frustrated, too overstimulated, too exhausted.

"Kumquat," he said again, softer this time, like he was trying to remind me.

I clenched my jaw, my body stiffening, my heartbeat hammering in my ears.

"It's not working!" I yelled at him.

I wanted him to stop saying it. I wanted him to stop looking at me like that. I wanted out of this moment—this feeling that was just making me feel like the worst mom.

We had come up with it together, our little strategy to help me catch myself when I was losing it, especially at bedtime. I had been struggling so much to stay calm, and we thought maybe a funny word would snap me out of it, remind me to take a breath before my frustration boiled over.

It was supposed to make me aware. It was supposed to help me stop.

But right now, all it was doing was making me even more irritated.

I remember the night we picked it. We were sitting in bed, the glow of my phone illuminating the room, the white noise machine humming softly in the background. I had been scrolling, looking for something that would help me. A parenting tip, a magic phrase, a technique that would make me feel like I wasn't failing every single night.

"What if we tried a code word to help me stay calm at bedtime?" I said out loud, not really expecting an answer.

My husband looked up from his book. "Like what?"

I hesitated, staring at the screen. The article I had pulled up was all about de-escalation tactics for parents, how a simple word could interrupt a downward spiral, shift the brain, and bring awareness in moments of stress.

"Something lighthearted," I murmured. "Something that won't feel like you're telling me to 'calm the f**k down.'"

He smiled, and so did I.

"Like what?" he asked again.

I shrugged. I wanted something that would make me pause, maybe even make me smile.

"Kumquat," I blurted out.

"Kumquat? The tiny Asian fruit?"

"Yeah. It sounds ridiculous. I bet I wouldn't be able to take myself too seriously if I heard it in the moment."

We both laughed, and for a second, I let myself believe it would work. Supposedly when I heard it, I would remember this moment—this feeling of hope, of possibility.

That I would remember who I wanted to be as a mother.

But now, as I stood in their loud bedroom, my patience hanging by a thread, there was no laughter.

Just the crushing weight of overwhelm.

Saying kumquat didn't undo the exhaustion that had been building inside me for years.

It didn't erase the overwhelm that had become my constant state of being.

It didn't stop the tidal wave of emotions that hit me every night when I was overstimulated, touched out, and running on fumes.

I wasn't just in a bad mood.

I was at my breaking point, and a single word, no matter how well-intended, wasn't going to save me.

Why Hacks Don't Heal

Hack	Heal
Force calm through willpower	Build calm through nervous system support
Apply surface fixes	Create root-cause transformation
Focus on doing more	Focus on feeling more grounded
Try to *get it right*	Learn to *meet yourself where you are*

Healing isn't about doing more.
It's about coming home to yourself.

I could feel the rage rising—the pressure, the heat behind my eyes, the tightness in my chest. My nerves felt raw, like I had been stretched so thin that even the smallest thing, like my husband saying that damn word, was too much.

I turned away from him and shut the door behind me.

I stood there, my back against the door, my breath coming in short, sharp bursts.

> *You don't need more hacks. You need more self-trust.*

I had nothing left to give.

That's when it hit me:
You can't hack your way out of survival mode.

You have to see it. Feel it. And choose a new way forward.

This was never about the kumquat.
It was about the moment before—
The moment I lost myself.

That's why Step 1 matters. Because catching yourself is the awareness, catching itself in real time—before the spiral takes over.

And this ... this was the beginning of something bigger.
Not just surviving motherhood—
But transforming it, **from the inside out.**

Are You in Stuck Parenting Hack Mode?

- Frantically Googling solutions
- Jumping from one tip or tactic to the next
- Feeling panicked when nothing seems to "work"
- Believing the next trick will finally fix everything

If you're stuck in hack mode, it doesn't mean you're weak. It means you're exhausted—and ready for something deeper.

MamaZen Moment

You Are Not a Project to Fix

Reflection:
Close your eyes.
Feel into the part of you that's trying so hard to get it right.
Place your hand over your heart and whisper:

I am not broken.

I am not a project.

I am a human being learning to breathe.

Reframe:
You don't need more tricks.
You need more trust—in yourself.

Practice:
The next time you feel that frantic *"I need to fix this"* urgency...

Pause.

Inhale deeply.

Exhale fully.

Then gently ask: *Do I really need to fix anything right now— or do I just need to feel it?*

Nina's Story

"After my last baby, I went through eclampsia, postpartum anxiety, depression, and months of insomnia. My whole self just turned inside out."

Nina tried everything the blogs recommended—routines, diet changes, self-care checklists—but none of it touched what was happening inside. Eight months later, she still felt like she was unraveling.

"With MamaZen, I finally felt understood. It reminded me this was temporary—and I wasn't alone."
—*Nina, MamaZen Member*

The moment she stopped trying to fix everything and focused on calming herself—that's when the peace finally came.

PART 2
The Shift Begins

CHAPTER 8

When the Fog Began to Lift

Before you can change anything, you have to notice it—gently, bravely, without judgment.

Awareness is the foundation of this step. Catching yourself is the moment you start to truly notice.

That's when you begin to see the pattern—instead of just surviving inside it.

I had reached my breaking point. I wasn't okay.

Two kids under three. Two tiny humans needing me every second of the day.

One crying, the other whining—both clinging.

No space.
No quiet.
No time to breathe.

I was outnumbered, overwhelmed, running on fumes.

And yet, the world expected me to handle it with grace—like this was just motherhood.

So they told me what they thought would help:

"You're doing great."
"It'll get easier."
"Just rest. Take a break. Find some time for yourself."

As if that was all it would take.

But how?

How do you take a break when you're the one keeping everything together?
How do you "rest" when the moment you sit down, someone needs you again?
How do you ask for help when you don't even know what kind of help you need?

I was drowning in the trenches of motherhood, and there was no one there to pull me out.

Not because they didn't care.

But because they didn't know how to help me either.

I was anxious.
I was stressed.
I was burned out.

I had been running on empty for years.

I thought I needed:

More sleep.
More patience.
A better routine.
A better execution plan.

But what I really needed was to change the way I was experiencing motherhood.

Because motherhood wasn't going to slow down, or magically become "easier."

The only thing I could change was how I felt inside.

I had spent all this time trying to control:

My baby's sleep pattern.
My kids' behavior.
My emotions.

**Step 1:
Catch Yourself**

- Notice when you're slipping into an old pattern
- Name it with honesty: "I'm overwhelmed." "I'm snapping." "I'm frozen."
- Interrupt the autopilot—with curiosity, not judgment
- Ground yourself: feel your feet, take one slow breath
- Remember: noticing *is* changing

Catching yourself is the beginning of rewiring yourself.

But control wasn't the answer. I needed to change the way my mind and my body responded to stress. And that moment—that breaking point—led me to realize something I never noticed before.

It wasn't some big aha moment. Nothing magical happened.
It was just one subtle shift. One second where I caught myself.
And in that second, I saw it—I had been running on autopilot.

I wasn't just exhausted and overwhelmed, I was stuck in a cycle. A cycle of stress, depletion, and guilt. A cycle that so many of us get trapped in without even realizing it.

Maybe you've felt it too. You wake up already overwhelmed, running through the endless mental checklist before your feet even hit the floor.

Maybe you spend your days trying to keep everything together, only to fall into bed at night feeling like you've failed—again.

And maybe, like me, you've convinced yourself that if you just push through, it will get easier. But here's the truth: it doesn't get easier. Not unless something changes. And the first step to change is seeing the pattern you've been stuck in.

That was my moment of awareness—the moment I finally understood that I didn't just need to survive motherhood. I needed a new way of experiencing it.

And now, reading this, you're probably having that moment too.

At first, awareness didn't seem like anything.

It didn't make my exhaustion disappear. It didn't erase the chaos or the weight I was carrying. It didn't give me the break I so desperately needed.

But it did change something.

It was like a crack of light breaking through a door that had been locked shut for years.

For so long, I had been in my experience—I was too close to it, too deep in the daily grind, too consumed by the demands of motherhood to even recognize what was happening.

But awareness pulled me out just enough to see the bigger picture.

Before that night, I thought my exhaustion was just part of the job. That my stress was normal. That my lack of patience was a personal failure.

But once I became aware of the cycle, I realized something:

I wasn't broken.
I wasn't failing.

I had just been operating on autopilot, running the same loop every single day without even realizing it.

> **5 Signs You're Catching Yourself**
>
> *(Even If It Doesn't Feel Like It Yet)*
>
> - You pause—*even for a second*—before reacting
> - You notice a pattern while it's happening
> - You name what you're feeling, even if it's after the fact
> - You soften your tone mid-sentence
> - You reflect afterward—not to shame yourself, but to learn
>
> *Progress is noticing the moment—even when you're still in it.*

And now that I saw it, I couldn't unsee it.

Our brains are designed for efficiency. Neuroscientists refer to this as the default mode network (DMN)—a system that helps automate repetitive thoughts and behaviors to conserve mental energy. This is why you don't have to consciously think about driving a familiar route or brushing your teeth; your brain already knows what to do.

But here's the problem: the brain doesn't just automate actions. It automates emotions, reactions, and stress responses too.

When we experience the same stress patterns over and over again, our brain strengthens the neural pathways associated with those reactions. This is called neuroplasticity—the brain's ability to rewire itself based on repeated behaviors. The more we repeat an emotional response—like feeling overwhelmed, snapping at our kids, or falling into guilt—the stronger that response becomes. It turns into a habit, something we do without even realizing it.

The result? We wake up already stressed. We react the same way to challenges. We fall into bed exhausted and defeated. And the next day, we do it all over again.

This is why awareness is so powerful. Because once we recognize that our thoughts and reactions are just conditioned patterns, we can begin to retrain our brains—breaking free from the automatic loops that keep us stuck.

The hardest part? When you're in it, you don't even know it's happening.

But when you step back—when you finally become aware—you start to see the pattern.

And that's when you can finally start to break it.

Take a moment and ask yourself:

Do I wake up feeling overwhelmed before the day even starts?
Do I feel like I'm constantly reacting instead of being in control?
Do I move through my days on autopilot, doing everything but feeling nothing?
Do I feel stuck in a cycle of stress, exhaustion, and guilt?

If you answered yes to any of these, I want you to know something:

It's not because you're failing. It's because your mind and body have been wired to react this way.

But now, you have the power to step back and see the cycle—and once you see it, you can begin to change it.

For the first time, I stopped blaming myself.

> **You can't change what you don't see.**

I wasn't a bad mom.
I wasn't weak or failing.
I was simply stuck in a pattern that I had never been taught how to break.

And that's why awareness is the first step.

Because until you see the pattern, you can't change it.

If you're reading this and thinking,

This is me. This is exactly how I feel.

Then take a deep breath, because this moment—*right here*—is important.

This is the moment where you stop believing that you just need to try harder.
This is the moment where you stop blaming yourself.
This is the moment where you start to see that you are *not* the problem—the cycle is.

And now that you see it, you have a choice. You can keep running on empty, hoping something shifts on its own. Or you can take the first steps toward something different.

I had spent so much time thinking that if I just figured it out on my own, things would get better. But the truth was, I didn't have the tools. I didn't know what to do next. I just knew I couldn't keep going the way I was.

And maybe that's where you are right now.

I know change feels impossible when you're exhausted. I know the idea of doing one more thing feels overwhelming. But here's the truth: change doesn't start with doing more. It starts with seeing things differently.

And that's what awareness gives you—the power to step outside the cycle and choose a new way forward.

MamaZen Moment

The Power of Noticing

Reflection:
Think back to the last time you reacted automatically.
What did you need most in that moment—punishment?
Or compassion?
Place your hand on your belly.
Breathe into the place where your reactions live.
Whisper: *I see you. I'm learning a new way.*

Reframe:
Awareness isn't weakness.
Awareness is where change begins.

Practice:
Today, notice just one reaction.
That's it.
Just notice.
Noticing is enough.

Amber's Story

Amber was deep in the toddler trenches—tantrums over the wrong cup, toys everywhere, constant noise. Most days felt like a cycle of yelling, apologizing, and then doing it all over again. She hated how she sounded, but no matter how hard she tried, she couldn't seem to stop.

Then one day, in the middle of a meltdown, something clicked. She heard herself yelling—and this time, she noticed. Not just the noise, but the pattern. The reaction. Hers.

It didn't mean she stayed calm after that.
But it was the first time she saw it happening while it was happening.
And that changed something.
And that gave her the power to change it.

CHAPTER 9

The Ripple Effect of Dysregulation

Don't mess them up! This thought ran through my mind more times a day than I could count.

It was the silent fear woven into every decision, every reaction, every interaction. The weight of knowing that what I did now would stay with them forever. That every moment had the power to shape them, to leave a mark.

So when it does happen, it is the worst feeling for every parent.

You yell at your child.

Their little body jolts, startled by the force of your voice.

Then they freeze.

Their eyes wide open lock on yours, unblinking, searching, unsure.

It isn't defiance. It isn't an attitude.

It is fear.

The kind of fear that reaches deep into their nervous system before their brain even has time to process it. The kind that makes their body react before their mind understands what's happening.

They just stand there, stiff and silent, shoulders rising, breath held.

And then—eventually—they cry.

Not an outburst. Not a tantrum.

A slow, trembling, heart-wrenching sob.

And in that moment, your body does the same thing.

Your chest tightens. Your throat burns. Your stomach feels knotted with regret.

You want to take it back.

To scoop them up, hold them close, tell them it wasn't their fault. That you were just tired. That you were overwhelmed. That you never wanted to make them feel that way.

But it had already happened.

No one has ever taught you how to regulate your own nervous system when you are drowning in exhaustion, overstimulation, and stress.

And that is the problem.

No one had ever taught *any* of us.

My dysregulation caused everyone in the house to become dysregulated.

Catching myself wasn't just about noticing my own reactions. It was about seeing the ripple effect they created—on my kids, my partner, on my entire family system.

Like a domino effect, my energy rippled outward—and suddenly, the entire home felt out of balance.

My baby sensed my stress and became more anxious and clingy.
My toddler fed off the tension, becoming defiant or extra sensitive.
My husband picked up on the energy, getting short-tempered or distant.

Everyone felt the shift.

It didn't matter that I was the one who was overstimulated. It didn't matter that I was the one drowning in mental exhaustion. The moment my nervous system went into overdrive, my family followed.

And instead of making things easier for me, it made everything so much harder.

Now, instead of just managing my own emotions, I had to help regulate everyone else from my own dysregulation.

It was exhausting.

Do you see the vicious cycle here?

I would get overwhelmed → my family would absorb it → now they were dysregulated too → and I would have to deal with their stress on top of mine.

And the worst part?

I didn't even realize I was the one setting the tone.

It took me years to see it. Years of wondering why my kids were so clingy, why they seemed to spiral at the worst moments, why my husband and I kept feeling like we were constantly *off*—not just as parents, but as partners.

I told myself they were just sensitive. I blamed it on bad sleep, a sugar rush, too much screen time.

But the reality was much harder to swallow.

How Your Energy Sets the Tone

- Your nervous system becomes your child's emotional environment
- A dysregulated parent often leads to a dysregulated child
- A calm parent creates a sense of safety and connection
- Your child doesn't just hear your words—they feel your energy
- Before they understand language, they understand *you*
- Your state becomes their emotional blueprint

You're not just managing behavior—you're modeling nervous system safety.

I was the common denominator. *I was the one who unknowingly set the emotional thermostat of our home.*

I thought I was just having a moment.

But what I didn't see was that my moment was spreading like wildfire.

And my kids? They were just trying to survive it.

Children don't know how to filter out their parent's energy.

They absorb it.

They mirror it.

And when their safe place—*me*—became unpredictable, their entire world felt unstable.

Their nervous systems weren't designed to regulate on their own. They relied on mine.

But how could I help them regulate ... if I never learned how to regulate myself?

The truth was, I didn't know how.

> **When Your Dysregulation Becomes Contagious**
>
> ▶ Your child becomes clingy, whiny, or defiant
> ▶ Your partner becomes reactive or emotionally distant
> ▶ You feel like you're holding everyone's emotions together—and falling apart inside
>
> *This isn't your fault. It's a sign your system is overloaded.*

I never saw my parents take a deep breath before responding. I never saw them pause when they got overwhelmed. I never heard them say, "I need a moment to calm down before I respond."

Regulating emotions wasn't something we grew up with.

For most of us, we were taught to stuff it down or let it out.

Either suppress it until it explodes, or explode and pretend it never happened.

Both felt terrible.

Neither was what I wanted to pass down to my kids.

So I had to ask myself—

If I didn't want to pass down this pattern, how do I break it?

And the answer?

It wasn't about controlling my kids.

It wasn't about making them listen, behave, or stop pushing my buttons.

It was about learning to regulate myself first.

> *Your child can't out-regulate you. They can only mirror you.*

Because the truth is, kids don't learn emotional regulation by being told what to do. They learn it by watching us. By feeling us. By absorbing the energy we bring into the room.

So if I wanted my home to feel calmer, more connected, more at peace…

I had to start with myself. A dysregulated parent can't regulate a child.

We expect our kids to calm down when they're upset.
To listen when they're frustrated.
To stop yelling when they're overwhelmed.

But how can they do that—when we, their parents, can't even do it ourselves?

We tell them to take deep breaths, to use their words, to walk away when they're mad.
Yet we find ourselves snapping, raising our voices, reacting on impulse.

Because when we're stuck in fight-or-flight, we aren't modeling calm—we're modeling stress.

When we snap at them to "calm down!"—they absorb our tension.

When we yell "stop yelling!"—we're showing them that yelling is how we handle frustration.

When we react without thinking—they learn to react without thinking, too.

Our words become meaningless when our actions tell a different story.

Children don't learn regulation from being told to calm down.

They learn it from watching *us* regulate ourselves.

They study us.

They absorb us.
They become us.

So I had to go first.

I had to learn how to regulate myself before I could ever expect my children to do the same.

This wasn't just about handling meltdowns better.

It wasn't about getting my kids to behave or listen or stop fighting.

It was about changing the way I existed in my home.

The energy I brought into the room.
The way I responded when I felt overwhelmed.
The example I set in the hardest, messiest moments of parenting.

Because whether I liked it or not…

I was teaching my kids how to regulate themselves.

Every single time I reacted, I was shaping the way my kids would handle their emotions for the rest of their life.

Would they learn that big feelings meant chaos, yelling, and shutting down?
Or would they learn that feelings were safe, manageable, and temporary?

Would they learn to explode when overwhelmed? Or to take a moment, breathe, and respond with clarity?

The truth hit me like a wave:

If I didn't break the cycle, I would only pass it down. And that was something I couldn't live with.

The next step in the MamaZen Method—Hit Pause—will be the beginning of ending your dysregulation.

> **MamaZen Moment**
>
> *The Thermostat Shift*
>
> **Reflection:**
> Close your eyes.
> Picture yourself as the emotional thermostat in your home.
> No judgment—just awareness.
> Ask yourself:
> *What emotional temperature am I setting most often?*
>
> **Reframe:**
> I'm not responsible for everyone's emotions.
> But I *am* responsible for the energy I bring.
>
> **Practice:**
> Today, pause just once.
> Instead of trying to regulate everyone else,
> regulate yourself first.

Maya's Story

Maya always thought her kids were just sensitive. The meltdowns, the clinginess, the tension in the house—it all felt like part of the job. But after one rough morning, when she snapped at her toddler and watched the entire household spiral within minutes, something clicked. Her energy wasn't just hers—it was contagious. She realized she wasn't just reacting to the chaos. She was creating it.

That day, she began making space for herself—just a few quiet minutes to reset.

"Some days, I still get overwhelmed. But now, I have a way to calm myself first—so I can help them calm down too."
—*Maya, MamaZen Member*

CHAPTER 10

Before You Snap

Once I finally saw the cycle I was stuck in, I knew something had to change. So I tried it all—talk therapy, yoga, meditation—anything that promised relief.

Therapy didn't help at all, it just made me replay over and over why I was so angry, which made me more anxious about my situation, which created more negative neural connections.

Meditation was impossible—I failed at meditating because I was already drowning in stress and anxiety and the last thing I wanted was to sit in it longer.

Most things we're told to try—talk therapy, parenting hacks, deep breathing, yoga, journaling, self-help books, podcasts—they only work on the *conscious* mind.
But your triggers?
Your stress responses, your guilt, your automatic reactions?
Those live deep in the *subconscious*—which controls 85% of your mind's power.

That's why no matter how many parenting tips you read…
No matter how often you tell yourself to "stay calm"…
Your body still reacts.
Because logic alone can't rewire a survival pattern.

I didn't want to admit it, but I was hitting a wall.

I had tried everything they say is supposed to help—but none of it actually worked.

I still felt anxious.
Still on edge.
Still one meltdown away from completely snapping.

And this is where Step 2 of the MamaZen Method begins: *The Pause.*
The moment you move from simply noticing your patterns… to doing something about them.

That split-second between your trigger and your reaction.
The space where everything can shift—if you know how to find it.

I was on the couch, crying after a long day and an endless bedtime, when my husband walked through the door.

Here is the irony in the whole story—my husband, Jake, is a Clinical Hypnotherapist.

He helps people overcome anxiety, anger, stress, and habits that are keeping them stuck. And he's really good at it—his clients were transforming their lives in just a few sessions.

And yet—there I was, crying on the couch, anxious and unraveling—and it had never once occurred to me to ask him for help.

I thought I just had to figure it out on my own. He thought I had a built-in motherhood AI tool and that I knew what to do. We both thought this was just how motherhood was supposed to feel.

But that night I told him straight up:
"You know, just like your clients, I need help too."

"Do you remember the mom of six kids you helped overcome her anxiety and rage? The one who went from constantly yelling to feeling so calm that her husband actually got concerned?" I asked my husband

My voice cracked as I swallowed back the lump in my throat.

"I'm tired of hearing how much you're helping everyone else. What about me?"

And for the first time, he listened—not as my husband, but as a professional.

I told him everything as raw and real as I could. How exhausted I was and how the weight of motherhood felt like too much. I told him how my mind never stopped racing and my patience was paper-thin. I shared how I was always on edge, always one hard moment away from snapping.

I asked him for help—not just with the kids, not just around the house—but inside my own mind.

And he listened.

He didn't try to reassure me. He didn't tell me I was doing great or that everything would be fine.

He just saw me.

Finally, he got it. Instead of trying to fix me, instead of offering advice or telling me it would get better, he did something else.

He created something for me.

That same night, he went back to his office and recorded audio sessions—just for me—designed to help me reset my mind, release the stress I was holding, and actually feel different instead of just pushing through.

I didn't know it yet, but those recordings would be the start of my transformation.

The next day, I began to listen.

And I cried.

A lot.

Not because I was sad, but because for the first time, I felt like I had found what I had been searching for—relief.

Relief from the mental load.
Relief from the racing thoughts.
Relief from the burnout that had consumed me for so long.

I felt like I was slowly coming back to life.

I felt calm.

It was something that had felt completely out of reach for years.

Cognitive hypnotherapy helped me realize:
My reactions weren't actually about my kids.
My stress wasn't just about what was happening in the moment.
My emotions weren't random—they were patterns.
Patterns my brain had been following for years.

And the best part?
Those patterns could be changed. (Remember, neuroplasticity?)

I didn't have to "try harder" to be calm. I just had to train my brain to respond differently.

I was determined to beat these feelings of drowning in the trenches of motherhood, plus I love my husband's hypnotic voice, and so I listened to my recordings every day.

And then something happened.

A few weeks in, I was tested.
We were running late. The girls were fighting on the stairs while putting their shoes on. The noise, the stress, the pressure—it was all there, the same as always.
I felt it rising, that familiar rage climbing up my chest, ready to explode.
But this time, something was different. There was a pause.

A space between the trigger and my reaction.

And in that pause, I had a choice.

I could react the way I always had—snapping, yelling, letting the stress take over.

Or I could do something different.

I chose the calm path. I took a breath, softened my shoulders, and spoke to my kids instead of reacting to them.

They paused and looked at me, confused for a second.

They felt the shift.

> **What Hitting Pause Actually Looks Like**
>
> - Taking one deep breath before reacting
> - Brief eye contact without needing to say anything
> - Placing your hand on your chest instead of snapping
> - Walking out of the room to reset
> - Saying softly: "I need a minute"
>
> *It's not about doing it perfectly. It's about creating space.*

And this is exactly how the pause happens.

At first, the pause might feel impossible. When you're deep in a moment of stress, it feels like everything is moving too fast. The triggers hit, your body reacts, and the next thing you know, the words have already left your mouth. The regret comes just as quickly, hitting you like a wave—but by then, it's already too late.

That's why this step is so important.

The pause isn't about perfection. It's not about never getting frustrated or never raising your voice. It's about reclaiming those tiny moments before you react—those split seconds where everything feels like it's about to spiral out of control.

Without the pause, you are stuck in autopilot, letting emotions drive the moment. With the pause, you give yourself a chance to shift.

A breath.
A beat.
A tiny, almost imperceptible moment where you have a choice.

> **Why Pausing Feels Hard at First**
>
> - Your brain is wired to react fast—pausing interrupts the loop
> - Pausing feels awkward because you're rewriting your brain
> - Every pause you take builds a new emotional pathway
>
> *The pause is your superpower—quiet, steady, and conscious.*

The pause doesn't have to be long.
It doesn't have to be flawless.
It doesn't mean you won't feel frustration or irritation.
It simply means you create *space*.

Space between the trigger and your reaction to recognize what's happening inside of you before you let it spill out onto your child.

Space to ask yourself:
"What kind of parent do I want to be at this moment?"

Maybe you still raise your voice, but instead of a full-blown outburst, you catch yourself mid-sentence and soften.

Maybe you still feel the frustration, but instead of slamming the door or barking commands, you take a deep breath first.

Maybe you still feel the urge to snap, but instead of reacting automatically, you step back—even if just for a second.

> *The pause doesn't have to be long. It just has to happen.*

The pause gives you that power.

At first, it may only happen once in a while.

But, then, it happens more often.

And all of a sudden one day, you realize something incredible—

You're *choosing* calm.
You're *choosing* connection over reaction.
You're *choosing* a different way.

And for the first time in a long time, *I felt in control again.*

The more I used the audio sessions, I began to notice that the things that used to push me to the edge didn't hit quite as hard.

I realized what I was experiencing wasn't just mindfulness. It wasn't just relaxation. It was hypnotherapy—working deep in my subconscious.

It was retraining my mind to break out of survival mode … and finally stop reacting on autopilot.

The transformation felt so good that I wanted more.

I asked my husband to make more sessions for me—for different emotions, for different triggers, for the overwhelming moments I faced every single day.

I wanted to listen.
I needed to listen.

Not in the desperate, exhausted way I had once clung to parenting books and tips that never seemed to work. But in a way that felt nourishing. Like something inside me had been starving, and I was finally feeding it what it needed.

It was so empowering. The more I listened, the more I changed.

Not overnight. Not in some dramatic, movie-style transformation.

But in the tiny, almost imperceptible ways that add up over time.

I was softer.
I was more patient.
I was emotionally rejuvenated.

And it wasn't because I had forced myself to be. It wasn't because I had memorized some script or learned a new technique.

It was because I had started changing from the inside out. The anger, the frustration, the overwhelm—they weren't controlling me anymore. I was learning how to break the cycle.

How to pause.

How to choose who I wanted to be, instead of feeling trapped in the same reactions, over and over again.

That was an empowering transformation.
That was the real breakthrough.

I don't know why I wasn't thinking of using hypnotherapy that whole time.

It was right there. Right in front of me.

Maybe it was because it was too close to me. Like the shoemaker whose kids have no shoes. Or the hairstylist whose roots are always grown out.

But when the lightbulb finally went on, I felt this rush of hope.

I was excited about the progress I was making and it happened fast. For the first time in forever, my mind wasn't anxious. I wasn't mentally going over tomorrow's to-do list. I wasn't planning, worrying, or replaying the day's stress on an endless loop.

It was like my entire nervous system exhaled.

I was just there. Present. Open. At peace.

With hypnotherapy, I didn't have to try. I just had to listen.

No effort. No focus. No doing it "right."

It wasn't magic—it was science.

Hypnotherapy shifts your brain into a deeply relaxed state, where real change can actually happen.

It's like updating the software in your mind—so you're not stuck running the same stress-filled program on repeat.
The patterns you've been reacting from for years?
You can rewrite them—without force, without effort.
Just by listening.

That's why hypnotherapy isn't just a trend—it's the future of mental wellness.

People don't just want to "cope" with stress anymore.
They want to *actually* feel better.

They're done with band-aid solutions.
They want something that truly changes the way they think, feel, and react.

And I was so grateful I finally found my way to it.

Because the irritation still rose.
The anxiety still crept in.
But instead of falling into a full-blown episode, I could *hit pause*.

This was a complete transformation of my inner state.

And that inner state?

That's where **Step 3 of the MamaZen Method begins:** *Calm Your Core.*

MamaZen Moment

One Breath Between You and the Storm

Reflection:

Think of a moment today when you felt stress rising.

Now, visualize pausing—just for a breath.

Ask yourself:

What shifted in me when I paused?

Reframe:

Power isn't about controlling everything.

Power is the pause that lets you choose differently.

Practice:

Today, when your child tests your patience (because they will)...

silently whisper to yourself:

Pause first. Then choose.

Lena's Story

Mornings were always chaos for Lena—shoes missing, kids yelling, her own voice rising before 8 a.m. She'd start the day already overwhelmed, already regretting how she reacted.

She had tried everything: better routines, waking up earlier, deep breathing. But nothing touched the panic she felt once things started spiraling.

Then one morning, after another meltdown—hers, not the kids'—she finally noticed it. The way her body tensed. The way her voice rose. The way it all felt automatic.

"I didn't want to yell, but it was like I couldn't stop myself. That morning, I used this method—and it gave me just enough space to catch it. Just enough to stay with myself instead of losing it."
—*Lena, Mama of Two*

And for once, she wasn't just surviving the morning—she was moving through it with calm.

PART 3

Rewiring from the Inside Out

CHAPTER 11

Rewiring Your Nervous System

This is **Step 3 of the MamaZen Method: Calm Your Core.** Because you can't parent calmly when your body thinks it's in danger.

So why does staying calm feel so impossible?

You don't wake up in the morning planning to lose your patience.

You don't open your eyes and think: *Today, I'm going to snap at my kids.*
If anything, you tell yourself the opposite.

Today, I'll be calmer.
Today, I won't let the little things get to me.
Today, I'll handle things better.

And yet, the day begins.

The whining. The messes. The constant interruptions.

You take a deep breath, remind yourself to stay patient.

Then the fighting starts. Someone spills their juice. Someone else is refusing to put their shoes on.

You hold it in.

Then the crying begins. The pushing, more crying, the endless demands for your attention.

You try to keep your voice steady. Try to stay composed.

But the stress keeps building.

And suddenly—

You snap.

Your heart races.
Your breathing gets shallow.
Your body tenses.

And before you even have time to think, before you even realize what's happening—
You explode.

Not because you're a bad parent.
Not because you don't love your kids.

You're not weak. You're not broken.

It happens because your nervous system is in survival mode.

At that moment, your body isn't processing reality.

It's not thinking logically.

It's just reacting.

Fight, flight, freeze.

Your brain sees chaos, and it sounds the alarm: *Danger. Overload. Threat detected.*

And in that split second, your nervous system takes over.

Not the version of you that knows better.
Not the version of you that wants to respond with patience.
But the version of you that is wired for survival.

> **What Survival Mode Feels Like for Moms**
>
> - Racing heart
> - Shallow breathing (often unnoticed)
> - Snapping over things that feel small
> - Feeling like you might lose it over nothing
> - Constant tension in your shoulders or jaw
>
> *If your body feels on edge all day, it's not in your head—it's in your system.*

This is why it happens so fast—before you even have time to stop yourself.

Calm parenting isn't about trying harder or willpower—it's about calming your core. Because when your body is stuck in stress mode, when your nervous system is running on overdrive, no amount of *trying harder* will make you feel calm.

It will always feel like you're fighting against yourself because in that moment—you are.

You can't parent calmly from a place of constant stress.
You can't be present, patient, or responsive if your nervous system is always running on overdrive.

And yet, most of us are stuck in a cycle of chronic dysregulation—
We wake up already exhausted.
We run through our days overstimulated, overwhelmed, and overstretched.
We end up reacting instead of responding.

Not because we want to.
Not because we don't love our kids.
But because our nervous system is trapped in a state of fight, flight, or freeze.

> **Why Trying Harder Doesn't Work**
>
> ▸ Logic shuts down in fight-or-flight
> ▸ You can't "positive think" your way out of dysregulation
> ▸ You need physiological resets—not just willpower
>
> *Calm starts in the body, not in the mind.*

Trying to be patient while dysregulated is like trying to stay dry in a thunderstorm.

Good intentions aren't enough—you need the right tools to shift your nervous system *before* you hit overload. That's what makes the difference between snapping ... and staying steady.

The next time you feel yourself spiraling—when the heat rises in your chest, your jaw tightens, and the urge to yell takes over—catch yourself. Pause.

Even two seconds can be enough.
That tiny interruption can stop the automatic reaction and create just enough space to choose differently.

When your nervous system is dysregulated, your breath becomes short and shallow.
To shift out of survival mode, you need to breathe in a way that tells your body: *you're safe now.*

Here is a very simple way to reset, but you need to do it right.

Try this: The Big Sigh (Physiological Sigh)

- Inhale deeply through your nose—expand your stomach way out while you breathe in

- Take a *second* tiny sip of air at the top of your breath to fill up your lungs even more

- Exhale slowly through your mouth, lips pursed like you're blowing up a balloon

- Feel your system soften—even just a little

This helps activate your parasympathetic nervous system, signaling to your body that it's safe to calm down.

Now, *get out of your head and into your body.*

Stress lives in your body, not just your mind.

If you feel yourself losing control, do something physical to shift your state:

- Shake out your hands.
- Splash cold water on your face.
- Step outside and take a deep breath of fresh air.
- Press your feet firmly into the ground and notice how they feel.

Another easy way to interrupt stress and feel grounded is the 5-4-3-2-1 method. It will help bring your brain back to the present moment instead of being hijacked by stress.

- Name **5** things you can see.
- Name **4** things you can feel.
- Name **3** things you can hear.
- Name **2** things you can smell.
- Name **1** thing you can taste.

This method works because it disrupts the stress cycle by shifting your focus away from overwhelming emotions and into the present moment. It engages your senses, grounding you in reality instead of the whirlwind of anxiety or frustration. By actively noticing your surroundings, you give your nervous system a signal that you are safe, helping to bring a sense of calm and control back to your mind and body.

Another great tool is narrating what's happening to yourself. When your nervous system is dysregulated, your brain moves into survival mode, and you lose access to your rational thinking.

Name what's happening:

I feel overwhelmed right now, but this moment will pass.

My child is struggling, not giving me a hard time.

I can take a deep breath before I respond.

This reminds your brain that you are in control of your response—not your stress.

In the heat of the moment, it's easy to think that nervous system regulation is just about calming down when you feel overwhelmed. And while those in-the-moment strategies are essential, they're just scratching the surface of full nervous system regulation.

Real regulation is a long-term game.

It's not just about stopping yourself from snapping at your kids today.

It's about rewiring your entire stress response so that you don't feel like you're on the edge every single day.

It's about building a foundation where stress doesn't automatically lead to overwhelm, where frustration doesn't instantly trigger fight-or-flight, and where parenting feels lighter—not because your kids are perfect, but because your nervous system is resilient.

Many of us are walking around with chronically dysregulated nervous systems without even realizing it.

We've lived in fight-or-flight for so long that it feels normal.

We wake up already feeling behind.
We rush through the day, constantly overstimulated.
We carry the weight of invisible mental loads, never truly resting.
We move from one crisis to the next, always waiting for the next meltdown, the next mess, the next thing to go wrong.

And we wonder why we snap.

But here's the truth: You can't pour from an empty cup—but most parents don't even know what a full cup feels like.

When your baseline is stress, it doesn't take much to push you over the edge. That's why little things—spilled milk, whining, bedtime battles—feel so big.

> *Calm isn't something you think your way into. It's something you practice your way into.*

Because they aren't just about the moment.

They're stacking on top of years of unprocessed stress, exhaustion, and depletion.

The work of long-term nervous system regulation isn't just about handling stress in the moment. It's about lowering your baseline stress so that it takes more to push you over the edge.

It's about retraining your body to feel safe, even when life is messy.

If you want parenting to feel easier—not because your kids suddenly behave differently, but because *you* respond differently—it starts with the deeper work of nervous system regulation. Because when your nervous system is steady, your reactions shift, your patience grows, and everything starts to feel lighter.

This means prioritizing daily habits that help shift you out of chronic stress and into a more balanced, resilient state.

Your nervous system needs a buffer from the constant demands of parenting.

Even five minutes a day of intentional stillness—deep breathing, journaling, or just sitting in silence—can help rewire your baseline from stress to calm.

Release the stress that is trapped in your body. Gentle movement like walking, stretching, yoga, or dancing help signal to your nervous system that it's safe to release stored tension.

Don't wait until you're overwhelmed to try and calm down. Build proactive habits that keep your nervous system steady throughout the day—taking deep breaths in the morning, grounding yourself before transitions, drinking water, and getting outside.

Modern life is loud, fast, and chaotic, and our nervous systems weren't built for constant pings, notifications, background noise, and clutter.

- Reduce unnecessary stressors where you can.

- Build moments of quiet into your day.
- Cut back on screen time and social media if it leaves you feeling drained.
- Make sleep, hydration, and real downtime non-negotiable—not just for your kids, but for yourself.

You will have hard days. You will still lose your patience sometimes. That's part of being human.

The goal isn't perfection, the goal is awareness.
Because awareness is what gives you the power to pause, reset, and try again—with more intention and less guilt.

And when you do mess up, repair with your kids and remind yourself:

I'm learning.
I'm growing.
And that's enough.

I used to think motherhood needed to change for me to feel better. But I've already learned it was never about fixing motherhood—it was about learning to regulate myself.

Now, when things spiral, I don't go searching for control—I go inward.

Because the calmer I become, the less chaos there is to fight.

I didn't need my kids to behave perfectly to feel calm.
I didn't need my house to be spotless to feel at peace.
I didn't need everything to go my way to feel grounded.

I just needed to know how to regulate myself—because the way *I* show up shapes the way my kids learn to be in the world.

Remember, our kids don't learn regulation by being told to calm down.
They learn it by watching us.

When they see us:

- Breathe through frustration

- Pause before reacting

- Stay steady even in the chaos

That's how they learn to stay calm too.
Because this isn't just about calming down in the moment.

This is about breaking the cycle.

It's about creating homes where emotional safety is the norm—not the exception.
Where our kids don't have to unlearn what they lived through.
And no, you don't have to be perfect at calming down instantly.
You just have to start giving your nervous system new experiences—one breath, one choice at a time.

But breaking the cycle isn't just about what you do in the heat of the moment.
It's about understanding *why* the heat even rises in the first place.
Because the deeper work of regulation doesn't stop in the present—it pulls you into the past.

Back to the places where your patterns were formed.
The reactions you dislike most in yourself didn't start with your kids. They started long before you ever became a parent.

And that's where **Step 4 of the MamaZen Method begins: Heal from Your Past.**

> ### MamaZen Moment
>
> *Reset Your Inner Weather*
>
> **Reflection:**
> Think of a moment when you felt yourself spiral into stress.
> Without judgment, whisper to yourself:
> *My body is doing its best to protect me.*
>
> **Reframe:**
> I'm not broken.
> I'm learning a new way.
>
> **Practice: The Big Sigh**
> Inhale deeply through your nose.
> Take a second small sip of air at the top.
> Exhale slowly through your mouth—like you're blowing out a candle.
> Feel your system soften ... even just a little.

Jenna's Story

Jenna kept snapping by 9 a.m.—not because she was "mean," but because she was starting the day already in survival mode. She was waking up tense, reactive, and overstimulated before anything even went wrong.

She began each morning with breathwork combined with a MamaZen session on the app—a short practice to reset her nervous system before the chaos began.

"I've struggled with anxiety and depression most of my life. I've tried therapy and medication. But this method gave me something I hadn't felt before—calm in the moment. I feel lighter, more grounded, and more like myself."
—*Jenna, MamaZen Member*

CHAPTER 12

The Wound Beneath the Trigger

Growing up, I had an older abusive sister.

She hit me. She took my things. She made me feel powerless in my own home.

No one stepped in to protect me. No one told her to stop. No one acknowledged how much it hurt. I was left to fend for myself, to navigate the chaos alone, to absorb the unspoken lesson that my feelings didn't matter as much as keeping the peace.

I didn't realize how much that experience shaped me. I grew up, moved on, and told myself that the past was behind me. But trauma has a way of lingering beneath the surface, waiting for the right moment to resurface. I never questioned whether those wounds would follow me into motherhood. I assumed they were gone.

But the truth was, they weren't gone. They were buried—waiting. And when I became a mother, when my own children started fighting, everything I had suppressed came flooding back.

I wanted nothing more than for my two girls to be close—to grow up as each other's safe place, to have a bond that would last a lifetime. I wanted them to love and support one another, to laugh together, to lean on each other through life's ups and downs. More than anything, I wanted to break the toxic sibling dynamic I grew up with.

But instead, they fought.

They grabbed each other's toys, their small hands yanking and pulling as if winning the battle meant everything. They pushed and hit, their frustration exploding into physical clashes that felt too familiar. They screamed at each other, their words sharp and cutting, filled with blame and resentment.

And something inside me raged.

To me, it wasn't just sibling rivalry. It was taking me back to the moments I didn't feel safe. It wasn't just a normal part of childhood, something they'd outgrow. It was something I had lived through, something that had shaped me, something that had left scars I was still carrying.

Every scream, every shove, every moment of tension between them wasn't just about them. It was about the child in me who was still waiting to feel safe.
It was about the wounds I thought I had buried. It was about the years of feeling unprotected, unheard, and completely alone.

And that's the thing about triggers—they're rarely about the present moment.

They're echoes.
Old pain, dressed in new clothes.
And when that pain gets activated, it doesn't matter how much you love your kids—your body still goes into defense.

That's why the first three steps of the MamaZen Method matter so much.
You can't change what you don't recognize (*Step 1: Catch Yourself*).
You can't rewrite a story if you don't interrupt it (*Step 2: Hit Pause*).
And you can't show up calmly if your nervous system is still screaming (*Step 3: Calm Your Core*).

But even those tools only take you so far.
Because to truly change your patterns, you have to go deeper.
You have to understand where they came from.

That's where Step 4 begins: Heal from Your Past.

What I really wanted was to stop my kids' interactions from turning into what I had lived through.

I wanted to protect them from the pain I had felt, to make sure history never repeats itself in my home.

But instead of handling it calmly, I became the bully in those moments.

I yelled.
I blamed.
I took sides.

I thought I was protecting them, but in reality it was quite the opposite, I was just repeating the cycle of aggression in a different form.

And when I realized this, it hit me hard.

I wasn't stopping the cycle.
I was continuing it.
I was letting my past pain control my present reactions.
I was bringing my childhood wounds into their childhood, without meaning to, without even realizing it.

I wasn't reacting to my kids. I was reliving something I never had the tools to process and overcome.

It wasn't their fights that triggered me. It was my past.
I wasn't reacting to them. I was reacting to myself.
To the little girl inside me who never felt protected.
To the memories of fights that never ended in love or resolution.

I had spent my entire life believing that if someone had just stepped in, if someone had just put a stop to it, I wouldn't have had to suffer so much. So when my own children fought, I felt an overwhelming need to control it—to fix it, to stop it, to make sure it didn't escalate.

But my way of stopping it was forceful. It wasn't about teaching them. It wasn't about helping them navigate conflict. It was about shutting it down as fast as possible so I wouldn't have to feel that pain again.

That's when I knew—I had to do something different.

Because my kids weren't my sister. And I wasn't a powerless child anymore.

I had the power to change the story.
I had the power to break the cycle.
I had the power to respond, instead of react.

But first, I had to heal.

I had to acknowledge my triggers, to recognize that my past was whispering in my ear, distorting my present. I had to learn how to regulate my emotions, to ground myself in the moment instead of being pulled back into old pain. I had to rewire the part of me that still saw conflict as a threat—so I could guide my children instead of reacting to them.

It wasn't easy.

At first, I had to physically stop myself from intervening in the way I used to. I had to pause, breathe, and ask myself: *Am I*

> **Signs You're Parenting From Past Pain**
>
> ▸ You overreact to sibling fights or rivalry
> ▸ Minor disobedience feels like a personal betrayal
> ▸ Your child's emotional outbursts feel terrifying—or enraging
> ▸ You feel a desperate need to control the situation instantly
> ▸ You're flooded with old emotions: fear, shame, helplessness
>
> *When your response feels bigger than the moment, it usually is.*

responding to them, or to my past? I had to sit with my discomfort, with the memories that surfaced, with the fear that if I didn't stop them immediately, things would spiral.

And then, I started changing how I approached their fights.

I stopped taking sides.
I stopped yelling.
I stopped treating every disagreement like a disaster waiting to happen.

Instead, I got curious.

I listened.
I watched.
I gave them space to figure it out.

And when they needed help, I guided rather than controlled.

As I changed, something amazing happened.

My kids still fought—but the fights were different.

They started resolving their conflicts instead of escalating them.
They started understanding each other instead of just reacting.
They started apologizing on their own.

And for the first time, I saw what real sibling connection looked like—not forced, not controlled, but genuine.

I also saw something even more important.

I saw myself becoming the mother I had always wanted to be.

A mother who wasn't ruled by her past.
A mother who could teach through presence, not punishment.
A mother who could hold space for emotions, not shut them down.

Because the truth is, healing isn't just about not repeating the past—it's about choosing something better.

And that's exactly what I was doing.

Now I invite you to ask yourself: Where might your reactions really be about you—not your child?

Maybe it's not sibling fights—maybe it's whining, messes, disobedience, or being ignored. Whatever it is, if your reaction feels bigger than the moment deserves, there's a reason.

You're not just responding to your child.
You're responding to something that's been living inside you for years.

These triggers are messengers. They point you to the wounds that still need attention. And when you begin to heal those wounds—not ignore them, not bury them—you stop handing them down.

> **You're Not Overreacting—You're Over-Remembering**
>
> ▶ *When big feelings arise, it's often because they were never fully processed the first time.*
>
> ▶ *What feels irrational now may actually be unprocessed then.*
>
> ▶ *Your nervous system remembers what your mind tried to forget.*

That's why a trigger can hijack you in an instant.

Because your brain isn't reacting to what's happening now.
It's reacting to something old—something it never got the chance to process.
It bypasses logic, which is why you can go from calm to overwhelmed in seconds.

In these moments, your nervous system is operating in survival mode, responding as if a past threat is happening all over again. Your body floods with stress hormones, your muscles tense, and your emotions surge—not because of the current situation, but because your brain has been trained to associate this experience with something painful from your past.

Your child not listening isn't just frustrating. It reminds you of the times you felt unheard as a child—when no one acknowledged your voice, when you were dismissed, when your needs were ignored. It's not just about this moment; it's about all the moments you longed to be seen and valued.

Your child whining isn't just annoying. It reminds you of when you were told to "stop crying," to "toughen up," to push down your feelings and be quiet. It stirs up the buried emotions of times when your own pain was minimized, when you learned that expressing your emotions was wrong or too much.

Your child talking back isn't just defiance. It reminds you of the strict authority you had to obey as a child—the moments when you weren't allowed to question, when disagreeing meant punishment, when you had to suppress your thoughts and feelings to stay safe. It reignites the helplessness of having no voice, no say, no control.

These old wounds shape how we parent, whether we realize it or not. They dictate the intensity of our reactions. They cloud our ability to see our children for who they are, rather than who our past conditioned us to believe they might become.

But the moment you recognize a trigger, you take back your power.
You create space between your past and your present.
You interrupt the cycle that was passed down to you.

Here's what that can look like:

Instead of reacting, you pause and center yourself.
Instead of repeating old patterns, you choose a new response.
Instead of carrying past pain into the future, you begin to heal.

> *Your child's tantrum isn't just about them. It's a mirror reflecting where you still need healing.*

Because your child isn't trying to hurt you. They're just being a child. And now, you have the opportunity to parent them from a place of healing, not hurt.

The good news is: triggers aren't permanent.
They can be rewired.
You are not stuck with them forever.

But healing them requires intention—and a process.

Here's where to begin:

Step 1: Identify Your Triggers

What are the specific moments that set you off the most?

Think back to the last time you lost your patience.
What was happening? What exactly triggered you?

Some of the most common parenting triggers include:

- Whining—that high-pitched, repetitive sound that makes your skin crawl.

- Not listening—having to ask five times before getting a response.

- Defiance or talking back—when your child challenges you instead of following instructions.

- Mess and chaos—the clutter, the spills, the never-ending noise.

- Sibling fighting—the arguing, the pushing, the constant bickering.

Now ask yourself:
Why does this moment affect me so deeply?
Why does whining make me want to scream?
Why does being ignored make me feel invisible?
Why does defiance feel like a personal attack?

This is where the rewiring begins—when you stop reacting blindly and start getting curious.
Because these reactions usually aren't just about the moment itself. They're about what the moment *represents*, based on your past.

Step 2: Find the Root

Once you've identified your biggest triggers, it's time to look beneath them.

Ask yourself:

- What does this moment remind me of?

- Did I feel this way as a child?

- Was I punished or ignored for expressing this kind of emotion?

- What was I taught about this behavior growing up?

Your childhood experiences created emotional blueprints—patterns of belief and reaction that still live inside you today. Your brain learned what to expect, what to fear, and how to protect you—even if that protection now shows up as yelling, shutting down, or losing control.

Step 3: Rewire the Response

This is where transformation happens.

Once you know the trigger and the root, you can choose a different path.
You can respond from your values, not your wounds.
You can take one breath. One pause. One new choice.

This doesn't mean you'll never get triggered again.
It means you'll stop being ruled by those triggers.

This is how you break the cycle—
Not just for yourself, but for your children too.

How the Past Shapes the Present

Here are a few examples of how past experiences can shape the way you respond to your child today:

Trigger	What It Reminds You Of	Root Cause
Your child ignores you when you ask them to do something.	You felt unseen or unheard as a child.	You learned that your voice didn't matter.
Your child throws a tantrum and cries over something small.	You were told to "suck it up" and stop crying.	You were conditioned to suppress emotions.
Your child talks back and refuses to follow directions.	You were punished for questioning authority.	You associate defiance with disrespect.
Your child makes a mess or doesn't clean up after themselves.	You grew up in a home where messiness was unacceptable.	You internalized that order equals control.

Once you make the connection between your trigger and its origin, you gain power over it.
You realize: *This reaction isn't actually about my child. It's about me. It's about a wound I've been carrying that never had the chance to fully heal.*

And once you can see it for what it is—you can change it.
You can stop the automatic pattern from repeating.

That's the heart of **Step 4: Rewiring Your Emotional Triggers**.
Now that you understand where they come from, you have the chance to respond from healing, not from habit.
This is where the cycle begins to break.

Now that you understand where your triggers come from, you have the power to break the pattern—and create a new response.

First, recognize the moment before it takes over.
When a trigger hits, your brain shifts into reaction mode.
But you have the power to pause the spiral.
Instead of snapping.
Instead of raising your voice.
Take a single, deep breath to reset.

In that space, remind yourself:

- *This is not about me.*

- *This is not my childhood.*

- *My child is not trying to hurt me.*

And then: validate your emotions—without acting on them.
Feeling triggered doesn't mean you're failing as a parent.
It means you're being asked to meet this moment with something new.

It's okay to feel frustrated.
It's okay to feel overwhelmed.
But your feelings don't have to control your response.

Try shifting your perspective:

- Instead of: *"Why do they always do this to me?"*
  Say: *"This moment is hard, but I'm in control of how I respond."*

- Instead of: *"My child is so disrespectful."*
  Say: *"They're testing boundaries like all kids do. This isn't personal."*

- Instead of: *"Why can't they just listen?!"*
  Say: *"They're still learning. I can guide them without losing control."*

- Instead of: *"They're being difficult on purpose."*
  Say: *"They're having a hard time, not giving me a hard time."*

- Instead of: *"They should know better by now."*
  Say: *"They're still developing. They need my guidance, not my frustration."*

These small shifts help you see your child as they are—
Not through the lens of your own past pain.

Your response should align with the parent you want to be.
So:

- Instead of snapping—exhale the tension.

- Instead of yelling—lower your voice.

- Instead of punishing—find a way to teach.

Each time you do this, you're not just stopping an old reaction—
You're rewiring your brain for something healthier and more intentional.

Rewiring your triggers isn't about perfection.
You will still have moments when you react, when you struggle, when old patterns pull you in.
But every time you pause...
Every time you choose a different response...
Every time you bring awareness to what's happening inside you...

You are changing the cycle.
You are shifting from reacting to your past—to responding in the present.
You are parenting from clarity instead of pain.

You are giving your children something you may not have had:
A parent who can handle conflict with calm.
A parent who can stay present in the storm.
A parent who leads with understanding—not fear.

And most importantly:

You are proving to yourself that you are not your triggers.
You are more than your past.
You are more than the wounds you've carried.

You have the power to rewrite how you show up—for your children, and for yourself.

This is how healing happens.
This is how the cycle ends.

Now it's time to choose how you want to show up.

That's where **Step 5 begins: Choose Your Energy**.

> **MamaZen Moment**
>
> *Seeing the Wound Beneath the Reaction*
>
> **Reflection:**
> Think of a moment recently when you felt triggered by your child.
> Gently ask yourself:
>
> *What did this moment remind me of?*
>
> **Reframe:**
>
> I am not the helpless child I once was.
> I have the power now to choose differently.

Practice:

Place a hand on your heart.

Say quietly:

I am safe.
My child is safe.
I can respond, not react.

Ally's Story

Ally grew up in an anxious home where everything felt unpredictable—so as a mom, she tried to control every detail: the schedule, the tone, the behavior. But when things didn't go as planned, her panic would take over.

She didn't realize she was recreating the fear she grew up in—until she started using this method and saw the pattern for what it really was: protection.

"When I feel anxious, my first reaction is to try and control everything around me. But using this method helps me come back to center. I feel calmer. More patient. More like the mom I want to be."
—*Ally, MamaZen Member*

Her healing began the moment she stopped trying to fix her child—and started soothing the frightened child inside herself.

CHAPTER 13

Setting Daily Intentions

"Your intention creates your reality."
— *Wayne Dyer*

Mornings used to feel like chaos.
Before I even got out of bed, my mind was already racing—thinking about everything that had to be done, already feeling behind.
The second my feet hit the floor, I was reacting.

Reacting to the mess.
Reacting to the noise.
Reacting to my kids' moods, their needs, their constant demands.

I felt like I had no control over my own day—just surviving until bedtime so I could finally get a break.

But here's what I've learned:
Emotional regulation isn't just about staying calm in the hard moments. It's about preparing yourself *before* those moments even happen.

You've caught yourself (Step 1), hit pause (Step 2), calmed your core (Step 3), and started healing the deeper emotional wounds (Step 4). Now it's time to get ahead of the chaos—by choosing your energy before the day begins.

This is Step 5 of the MamaZen Method: Choose Your Energy. You decide how you want to show up—before the world decides for you.

For the longest time, I thought regulating my emotions just meant trying harder in the moment.
"I won't yell today."
"I'll be more patient this time."

But no matter how hard I tried, it was never enough.
I was missing the step that comes before all of that: **setting an intention.**

Intention vs. Reaction

Without Intention	With Intention
Reacting to moods	Choosing your mood
Overwhelmed by chaos	Anchored by purpose
Guilt spirals	Graceful resets

*You can't always control the day—
but you can choose how you meet it.*

Because when I start my day on autopilot, I'm way more likely to fall back into old patterns. And if I wait until I'm overwhelmed to try and "calm down," it's already too late.

I've learned that I have to set my emotional state before the day even begins—that's what truly helps me show up the way I want to.

I stopped rolling out of bed and immediately stepping into stress.
I stopped letting my mood be dictated by my kids, my to-do list, or the state of my house.
I stopped letting the day control me—and started controlling how I showed up for it.

We often think of setting intentions as making a to-do list or planning out our day. But intention is so much more than that—it's about shaping your inner state, your mindset, not just your actions.

What if we could direct our emotional experience instead of being pulled by it?

This is where emotional regulation and intention intersect.

When you set an intention for your emotional state, you create a mental guide for how you want to feel and respond.

Instead of saying: *"I hope today goes smoothly,"* you decide: *"No matter what happens, I will approach today with patience and presence."*

Intentions become internal guardrails, helping you pause before reacting.

When your child refuses to put on their shoes? Instead of snapping, your intention reminds you: I guide with love and patience.

When you're overwhelmed by the mess in the kitchen? Your intention whispers: I focus on what matters.

When bedtime feels like a battle? Your intention grounds you: I am their calm in the storm.

Intention helps you regulate your emotions by giving you a choice in how to respond, rather than being hijacked by the moment.

Here are some simple steps you can take to set your intention for the day:

Before your day begins, take a deep breath and ask yourself:

How do I want to feel today?
How do I want to respond to challenges?

Choose one or two guiding emotions, like calm, patience, resilience, and throughout the day, repeat a phrase that aligns with your intention.

I am steady and grounded.
I choose calm over chaos.
I respond with love, not impulse.

When emotions rise, pause. This is where regulation comes in. Instead of reacting instantly, take a moment to reconnect with your intention. This could be through deep breathing, a short body scan, or simply repeating your anchor phrase.

Intention is not about making the day perfect—it's about helping you return to your emotional center when things go sideways. If you lose patience, get frustrated, or feel overwhelmed, remind yourself:

I can begin again in this moment.

Before I learned to set my emotional intention, my days felt like they were happening to me. I was just reacting to whatever came my way.

> **5 Morning Intention Ideas**
>
> ► Today I choose patience
> ► Today I protect my peace
> ► Today I lead with calm, not chaos
> ► Today I recognize small joys
> ► Today I breathe before reacting
>
> *Start your day with direction—not default.*

Now, I guide my day, rather than being swept up in it.

I choose my response.

This doesn't mean every day is perfect. It doesn't mean I never lose my patience or feel overwhelmed. But it does mean that I no longer feel like I'm drowning.

The key is to start the day before the day starts pulling at you.

Setting an intention doesn't have to take an hour.

In fact, it takes less than 5 minutes.

Here's how to do it:

Before getting out of bed and jumping into your to-do list, pause, take a deep breath.

Ask yourself: *How do I want to feel today?*

Instead of "I just need to get through today," start saying:

"Today I feel calm."

"Today I am patient."

"Today, I enjoy the little moments."

Decide on one guiding thought for the day. Some of my favorites are:

"I don't have to match their energy"

"Pause before reacting."

"This moment will pass."

Do one small action to center yourself, like:

Take 3 deep breaths.
Stretch for 30 seconds.
Drink your coffee before checking your phone.

It's not about having a perfect morning routine—it's about starting your day with intention instead of reaction.

There's real science behind why intention setting works.

Your brain has something called the Reticular Activating System (RAS)—a filter that decides what information is important. When you wake up in a stressed, reactive state, your brain notices more stress throughout the day. But when you set an intention, your brain starts filtering information differently.

If your intention is "I will pause before reacting," your brain actually helps you remember that in the moment.

If your intention is "I will find small moments of joy today," your brain starts noticing those moments more often.

It's like training your mind to focus on what you want to create, instead of just reacting to whatever happens.

> *You can't always choose what the day brings— but you can choose what you bring to the day.*

Let's be real—some days, no matter how much intention you set, things still feel hard.

So what do you do then? You reset your intention in the middle of the day.

If you feel yourself slipping into frustration or stress, pause for 30 seconds and do the following:

Close your eyes and take a deep long breath through your nose, hold it in for 2 seconds and exhale slowly through your mouth.

Remind yourself of your intention:

"I can reset at any time."

"This is just a moment, not the whole day."

"I am in control of how I respond."

Now, release the stress and move forward.

You don't have to wait until tomorrow for a fresh start.

You can choose a new intention at any moment.

That one change—from reacting to leading with intention—helped me shift how mornings and afternoons went.

Not because life got easier or my kids stopped being kids. But because I started taking control of how I experience motherhood.

And that's what I want for you, too.

Because once I started setting my emotional state with intention, I realized something even deeper was driving my reactions—the stories I was telling myself.

That inner script? It had way more power than I ever realized. So in the next chapter, we're going to start rewriting it—together.

Lead Your Day, Don't Chase It

Reflection:

Close your eyes.

Place one hand over your heart.

Ask yourself: *How do I want to feel today?*

Now breathe in that feeling—like a color filling your whole body.

Reframe:

Your energy is your child's weather system.

Set the forecast before the storm rolls in.

Practice:

Each morning, choose a power word:

love, connection, trust, ease, flow, grace...

Write it on a sticky note.

Place it where you'll see it—on the fridge, the mirror, your phone.

Let it guide you back whenever you drift from your center.

Samantha's Story

Samantha used to wake up already bracing for chaos. She'd leap into her day reactive, stressed, and always one step behind.

Then she tried something different. She began her mornings with a few quiet minutes—using this method to set her energy before the noise began.

"I felt like I was always yelling and on edge. But starting the day with this helped me feel calm, more present, and more like myself."
—*Samantha, MamaZen Member*

Her kids were still loud. The house was still messy. But she wasn't being pulled under anymore.

CHAPTER 14

Rewrite the Script

In Step 5, you learned to set your emotional tone each day—choosing your energy before the chaos begins.
Now we go deeper.
Because you can't parent with intention if you're still running on stories you didn't choose.

This is where **Step 6 of the MamaZen Method begins: Parent on Purpose.**
Because parenting with intention starts not just with what you do—but with what you believe.

When I was deep in the trenches of motherhood, I received all kinds of well-meaning advice. But the one that left the deepest sting was this:"Just reach out to another mom friend. It'll make you feel better."

And so I did.

I picked up the phone, desperate for some kind of relief. My body felt heavy with exhaustion, my mind cluttered with doubt. I needed to hear someone say, *"You're not alone."* I needed reassurance that what I was feeling—the overwhelm, the constant second-guessing, the crushing weight of motherhood—was normal.

I told my friend everything. How I was drowning in exhaustion. How I felt like I was failing every single day. How I didn't understand why this was so hard, why I couldn't seem to get it right. My voice cracked under the weight of my emotions, but I kept talking, hoping—praying—she would say, *"Oh my God, me too."*

Instead, she said:

"Really? We're doing great! Baby sleeps, eats, all good with us. Our toddler is sleeping in her bed all night long…"

I felt my stomach drop.

The silence on the line stretched. I forced a smile into my voice, muttered something about being happy for her, and hung up. And then, the weight of loneliness pressed down even harder.

I sat there staring at my phone, her words replaying in my head.

"Really? We're doing great!"

And just like that, the negative thoughts started racing.

What's wrong with me?
Why can't I handle this?
Why does everyone else seem to have it together?
Why am I the only one struggling?

The shame crept in, wrapping itself around me like a fog. Maybe I really was broken. Maybe I just wasn't cut out for this.

So I stopped reaching out to my close friends.
I kept everything inside, convinced no one would understand.
I smiled when I was supposed to, nodded along in conversations about how "amazing" motherhood was, and pretended I had it all together.

But inside, I was unraveling. And the more I buried it, the more anxious, irritable, and disconnected to my true self I became.

I knew I couldn't keep pretending forever.
On the outside, I smiled and held it together.
But it was eating me from the inside.

So I looked elsewhere—hoping that maybe, just maybe, some other mom would be as raw and honest as I was.
I wasn't willing to accept that this was just how motherhood had to feel.

I went to baby yoga, hoping for some relaxation and camaraderie.
I joined a Mommy and Me class, thinking maybe I'd find a

> **Common Motherhood Thought Traps**
>
> - I'm not doing enough
> - Other moms are better than me
> - I should be enjoying this more
> - Good moms don't need breaks
>
> When you believe these thoughts, you're not seeing the truth—you're seeing your conditioning.

kindred spirit. I even went to a few meetings my doula set up for the moms she had helped deliver, expecting open conversations about what we were all going through.

But no one mentioned anything about the reality of motherhood.

They talked about teething and sleep schedules. They swapped tips on baby carriers and the best organic snacks. They smiled, nodded, and carried on as if everything was fine. I played along, pretending I had it together, too.

Until one evening, it all came out. The moment I was hoping for finally arrived.

I was sitting with a group of about twelve moms at a long table, we were all chatty. Some had some wine and all of a sudden one of them finally broke the script.

She exhaled loudly, rubbed her temples, and said, *"I don't know what to do anymore. My boys don't listen, my husband annoys me, and I just … I've had enough."*

Silence.

And then, like a dam breaking, the truth started pouring out.

One mom said, "My patience is gone. I snap all the time, and I hate it." Another admitted, "I punish and take things away, but nothing changes."
Someone else added, "My husband acts like a kid—sometimes he makes more messes than the kids do."

The stories kept coming.

"I haven't slept through the night in over a year. I don't even know who I am anymore.'
"I've tried five different anxiety medications, and the side effects are killing me."
"The laundry piles are never-ending. My house is a disaster. I'm drowning."
"I love my kids, but sometimes I just want to run away for a weekend and not tell anyone where I'm going."

One by one, they opened up.

They weren't just sharing frustrations—they were unloading years of invisible burdens.

I sat there, listening, stunned.

I had spent so much time thinking I was alone in my struggles, that I was somehow failing at something everyone else seemed to handle effortlessly. But in that moment, I realized the truth:

None of us had it together.

Because parenting on purpose isn't about having it all figured out— It's about becoming aware of the beliefs and stories that shape how we show up.

So far, you've learned to:

- Catch yourself in the moment (Step 1)

- Hit pause (Step 2)
- Calm your nervous system (Step 3)
- Heal emotional triggers (Step 4)
- And choose your energy each day (Step 5)

And now, in **Step 6, it's time to Parent on Purpose**—by choosing what you believe instead of letting your old story run the show.

What unconscious stories have shaped how you see yourself as a mother?

Which ones are ready to be rewritten—so you can parent from clarity, not conditioning?

When you recognize the stories that shape your reactions, you gain the power to rewrite them—and lead your parenting with clarity, not conditioning.

Every one of us carries default thought patterns—the stories that shape how we see ourselves, our kids, and motherhood.

And these stories run in the background of our minds like a script we don't even realize we're following. A quiet, persistent narration that influences how we react, how we feel, and even how we define ourselves as mothers.

Some of the most common ones sound like this:

"I'm not doing enough."

No matter how much we do, there's always something left undone. The laundry, the meals, the to-do lists—always running behind, always feeling like we *should* be doing more.

"I'm not the mom my kids deserve."

We hold ourselves to impossible standards, convinced that every mistake, every impatient moment, every missed opportunity somehow means we're failing them.

"Other moms handle things better than I do."

We scroll through social media, watch other moms in the park, hear about their routines, their patience, their seemingly effortless ability to *do it all*—and we wonder why we can't seem to keep up.

"I should be enjoying this more."

Motherhood is *supposed* to be magical, right? We tell ourselves we should savor every moment, cherish the chaos, embrace the mess. And when we struggle—when we don't feel constant joy—we wonder if something is wrong with us.

"I just don't have the patience for this."

The tantrums, the whining, the constant demands—it feels like too much sometimes. We snap, we feel guilty, we promise to do better, and then the cycle repeats.

We don't question these thoughts, we just accept them as truth.

But what if they aren't?

What if they are just stories—ones we've unknowingly absorbed from the world around us? From the way we were raised, from societal expectations, from an idealized version of motherhood that doesn't actually exist?

Have you ever noticed how, on a bad day, everything feels worse?

You spill your coffee, your toddler throws a tantrum, you stub your toe—and suddenly, it feels like the entire day is unraveling. But was it really *that* bad? Or did your mind, already tuned into frustration, magnify every little thing that went wrong?

> **Truths to Replace Traps With**
>
> ▸ I am doing enough, even when it's hard
> ▸ No one is perfect—and that's not the goal
> ▸ It's okay for joy and exhaustion to coexist
> ▸ Good moms honor their own needs too
>
> *This is how you rewrite the script—one truth at a time.*

If you wake up thinking, *"Today is going to be stressful,"* your brain will look for stress all day long.

If you tell yourself, *"I'm exhausted, I can't handle this,"* every challenge will feel overwhelming.

If you think, *"My child never listens,"* your brain will zero in on every ignored request while completely overlooking the moments they *do* listen.

Your thoughts are filters, not facts.

They actively shape how you experience motherhood. And the more we repeat these thoughts, the stronger they become.

When we constantly tell ourselves we're failing, we begin to *feel* like failures—even when we're not.

When we believe we have no patience, we react with frustration instead of finding ways to build patience.

When we focus on what's going wrong, we miss everything that's going right.

This is why no amount of parenting hacks, deep breaths, or promises to "stay calm" actually work—*not for long anyway*—unless we deal with the real issue: the stories running in the background of our minds.

> **Your thoughts shape your parenting—until you learn to shape your thoughts.**

Because if your mind is filled with guilt, pressure, or thoughts like *"I'm failing,"* then it doesn't matter how patient you try to be or how much you remind yourself to "enjoy the moment"—you'll still feel like you're falling short.

This is why learning to **Parent on Purpose** is so crucial. If we want to change the way we experience motherhood, we have to start by changing the stories we tell ourselves.

Not through toxic positivity. Not by forcing ourselves to just think happy thoughts.

But by recognizing that our thoughts are not facts.

By shifting our focus to what's true:

We are doing more than we realize.
We are not the only ones struggling.
And we are not failing.

But if there's one story that shows up in almost every mom's mind—loud, constant, and hard to shake—

It's guilt.

Guilt is one of the heaviest emotional weights we bear as mothers—and yet, it serves no useful purpose. It doesn't guide us. It doesn't protect us. It just drains us.

We feel guilty about almost everything:

Guilty for how we gave birth.
Guilty for not breastfeeding—or not enjoying it.
Guilty for wanting time alone.
Guilty for losing our temper.
Guilty for not playing enough.
Guilty for screen time.
Guilty for needing a break.
Guilty for wanting more than just being "mom."

And on and on….

But here's the truth:

Guilt is not a sign that you love your kids. You already love them. Guilt is a sign that the expectations placed on you—by society, family, or your own inner critic—have become impossible.

We've been taught that guilt is productive. That it keeps us humble or makes us better. But guilt doesn't help you grow—it keeps you stuck. It's shame disguised as responsibility.

When we parent from guilt, we don't parent from truth—we parent from fear. We act out of desperation to *prove* we're good enough.

And the worst part?
Much of the guilt we carry isn't even ours—it's inherited.
From our own mothers. From culture. From the myth of the perfect mother we've internalized over time.

You've repeated those thoughts for years, often without realizing it. But the same way those old patterns were built—new ones can be formed.

Thought patterns are created through a cycle:

thought → emotion → behavior → reinforcement

It starts with a thought like: *"I'm not a good mom."*
That thought sparks an emotion—guilt, frustration, self-doubt. Then comes a behavior: you withdraw, snap, shut down, or spiral. And that reaction reinforces the original belief, strengthening the link in your brain.

This is why certain beliefs feel so deeply ingrained—they've been practiced so many times, they've become your brain's default setting.

You can interrupt this cycle and form new pathways—ones built on truth, not fear.

Here's how to create new positive thought patterns:

First, catch the thought.

Neuroscience shows that mindfulness—the practice of observing thoughts without judgment—activates the prefrontal cortex, the part of the brain responsible for rational thinking and emotional regulation.

When we notice our thoughts instead of automatically believing them, we weaken the old neural connections.

Instead of unconsciously spiraling into *"I can't handle this,"* notice the thought as it arises and label it: *"I'm having the thought that I can't handle this."* This small shift creates distance between you and the belief.

Next, challenge the thought.

Cognitive Behavioral Therapy (CBT) research shows that thoughts are not facts—they are often distorted perceptions shaped by past experiences, emotions, and biases.

Ask yourself:

Is this thought 100% true?
What evidence do I have against it?
Would I say this to a friend?

By challenging negative thoughts, you weaken their grip and begin forming a new neural response.

If you think, *"I'm failing as a mom,"* challenge it with:

"Would I say that to another mom who is trying her best? No. Then why am I saying it to myself?"

Now you are ready to *replace it with a new thought pattern.*

The brain thrives on repetition. To create new thought patterns, you must practice replacing old thoughts with new empowering ones.

This activates the hippocampus, which is responsible for learning, and strengthens new neural pathways over time.

Instead of thinking, *"I don't have enough patience,"* replace it with, *"I am learning patience every day."* Each time you make this shift, your brain reinforces the new pattern, making it easier over time.

Next, *use visualization and affirmations.* Studies show that visualization activates the same brain regions as real-life experiences. This means your brain starts treating your new thoughts as reality before they even happen.

Picture yourself handling a stressful situation with calm and confidence. Your brain begins strengthening neural pathways that support that reaction. Repeating truth-based affirmations helps embed new beliefs into your subconscious.

Instead of *"I'm always overwhelmed,"* practice: *"I can handle what today brings, one moment at a time."*

Practice taking small, consistent actions. Brain scans show that habitual actions reinforce neural pathways. This means that even small shifts in behavior—taking a deep breath before reacting, pausing before speaking, or writing down a positive thought—strengthen new patterns over time.

If you normally get frustrated when your child won't listen, practice responding differently just once.

If you tend to spiral into self-criticism, practice saying one kind thing to yourself daily.

Each action reinforces the new story you're telling your brain.

Changing thought patterns isn't about pretending challenges don't exist. It's about shifting how you respond to them.

By intentionally noticing, challenging, and replacing old beliefs, you can reshape your experience of motherhood—not by changing your circumstances, but by changing the way you *think* about them.

And over time, as these new patterns strengthen, your mind will naturally lean toward thoughts that empower you instead of thoughts that hold you back.

Your brain is not your enemy, it's your most powerful tool.

You can stop carrying the weight of *shoulds* and *not enoughs*.
You can stop believing the story that you're failing.
And stop seeing motherhood as a test you have to pass and start seeing it for what it really is—a journey. One where growth, mistakes, and messy moments are part of the process.

When you take away the self-judgment, the guilt, and the pressure to be perfect, you realize…

You were never the problem.
You were just stuck in a story that was never true.

And now, you get to write a new one—**by parenting on purpose.**

> **MamaZen Moment**

Rewrite the Story

Reflection:
Think of one harsh thought you often tell yourself.
Now soften it.
What would you say to a dear friend in the exact same situation?

Reframe:
Your inner voice shapes your outer experience.
Kindness toward yourself isn't indulgent—
it's essential.

Practice:
Each morning for one week, write one sentence of self-kindness.
Something like:
I love my kids with all my heart, and I bring so much to this family.
Then notice—what starts to shift inside you?

Amanda's Story

Amanda grew up in a loving but reactive home. Emotions were dismissed, yelling was normal, and calm parenting wasn't something she ever saw modeled. Without realizing it, she brought that same script into motherhood.

She found herself snapping, then feeling guilty, and thinking: *You're messing them up.*

Eventually, she began using the MamaZen app to change those deep patterns—not to fix her kids, but to stop repeating what she never chose.

"I didn't want to raise my kids the way I was raised. MamaZen helped me respond with empathy instead of reacting out of fear."
—Amanda, *MamaZen Mom of Two Boys*

Now, she's parenting with intention & purpose—not old conditioning.
She's not stuck in the script she inherited—she's writing a new one.

PART 4

Deepening the Practice

CHAPTER 15

Mindfulness Matters

This is the path you're beginning—to catch yourself in the moment, to calm your nervous system, to rewrite old triggers, to choose your energy, and to challenge the stories that were never yours to carry.

But there's one thread that weaves through every single step of the MamaZen Method.

And that thread is *mindfulness.*

Because none of this transformation sticks unless you learn how to live in the present.

You don't need more parenting tips or strategies.
You need space to think. To breathe. To *choose.*

That's what mindfulness gives you.

Mindfulness isn't about clearing your mind or sitting cross-legged in silence while your kids scream in the background.
It's not about perfection, detachment, or pretending to be calm.

It's about presence.

It's the moment you notice your shoulders are tense and decide to soften them.
It's the second you catch yourself about to yell—and pause instead.
It's the breath you take when everything in you wants to react, but something wiser in you wants to lead.

I used to think mindfulness was just another thing that only single people without kids practiced. You know, like waking up at 5 a.m. to journal and drink lemon water while meditating on a mountain. It was definitely not for me. I barely had time to sit, let alone be mindful.

But here's what I learned the hard way: mindfulness isn't about having more time. It's about changing how you experience the time you already have.

Living in a constant state of tension made my mind race from one worry to the next, always preparing for the worst.

Anxiety thrived in my thoughts—

What if I mess up my kids?
Am I failing my family?
I should have been more patient today.
I shouldn't have snapped at them.

It was constant. I was always five steps ahead, worrying about things that hadn't even happened yet, or stuck in the past, replaying the things I should have done differently. And because I wasn't living in the present, I was missing the only moment that actually mattered—the one happening right now.

Motherhood is a never-ending to-do list, which is why so many of us are drowning in anxiety. There's always something that needs to be done, someone who needs something, and a brain that refuses to shut off. And let's be honest, when you're responsible for tiny humans, the mental load is *crushing*.

For years, I kept waiting—for things to slow down, for my to-do list to shrink, for life to get easier. But it never did. It never does.

What changed wasn't my circumstances, but my ability to be present in them. Mindfulness shifted me from merely surviving life to actually living it.

> **Signs You're Parenting From Anxiety (Not Presence)**
>
> ▸ Constantly scanning for what's about to go wrong
> ▸ Reacting to future fears instead of present needs
> ▸ Struggling to enjoy moments, even when they're good
>
> *Anxiety pulls you into what-ifs. Mindfulness brings you back to what is.*

It's how you catch yourself without judgment.
It's how you pause before reacting.
It's how you lead with intention instead of anxiety.

This is also where mindfulness supports nearly every step of the MamaZen Method:

The MamaZen Parenting Method

- **Step 1: Catch Yourself**—noticing your thoughts and reactions without judgment.

- **Step 2: Hit Pause**—creating space between the feeling and the reaction.

- **Step 3: Calm Your Core**—mindfulness helps soothe your nervous system and send the signal: you're safe. It grounds you before emotions take over.

- **Step 4: Rewire Emotional Triggers**—mindfulness lets you catch the trigger in real time and say, "This isn't about my child. This is an old story." That awareness gives you the power to choose differently.

- **Step 5: Choose Your Energy**—noticing your emotional state and setting the tone before the day sets it for you.

- **Step 6: Parent on Purpose, Rewrite the Script**—mindfulness helps you observe the stories running in the background, so you can choose new beliefs and parent from clarity instead of conditioning.

Unlike mindfulness, anxiety only lives in the future.

It feeds on uncertainty—the "what-ifs" and worst-case scenarios that flood your mind. When you're lost in those thoughts, your brain sounds the alarm, reacting as if there's real danger—even when there's none. That's how anxiety hijacks your system, triggering fight-or-flight like you're being chased by a predator.

Mindfulness does the opposite.

It brings you back to the present—the only place where peace actually lives.

And research backs it up. Studies show that mindfulness lowers activity in the amygdala (your brain's fear center) and strengthens its connection to the prefrontal cortex—the part that helps you regulate emotions and make calm decisions (Taren et al., 2015).

And it's not just about the brain—your body feels it too.

One study found that medical students who practiced mindfulness had significantly lower cortisol levels—the hormone tied to stress overload (Turakitwanakan et al., 2013). Less cortisol means less tension, fewer meltdowns (yours and theirs), and a calmer nervous system overall.

Anxiety can't survive when your mind is anchored in the now. It loses its fuel—the what-ifs and worst-case scenarios.

> **Quick Ways to Practice Mindfulness (Even on Hard Days)**
>
> - Breathe slowly while folding laundry
> - Feel the water on your hands while doing dishes
> - Listen fully to your child's laugh—just 10 seconds of full presence
> - Notice the sun or wind on your face for one full breath
> - Place your hand on your heart and say, *"This moment is enough."*
>
> *Mindfulness lives in moments, not hours.*

Right here, right now, are you in danger?

Probably not.

And that's exactly why mindfulness works—it breaks the cycle of catastrophic thinking and brings your power back to the present moment.

By training your mind to return to the present, mindfulness becomes one of the most powerful tools to break anxiety's grip. It won't erase stress—but it will help you meet it with clarity instead of fear.

And trust me, this isn't about becoming a monk who never gets frustrated. It's about knowing what's happening in your mind and body—so you don't get dragged into the spiral of stress and overwhelm.

It's about recognizing when anxiety is running the show and choosing—yes, actually choosing—to take back control.

Mindfulness gives you the power to shift from chaos to clarity.

It helps you move from:

- **Reacting → Responding**
- **Overthinking → Observing**
- **Living in the future or past → Living in the present**
- **Feeling out of control → Feeling in control of your mindset**

It's like hitting a reset button.

Instead of spiraling into *what ifs*, mindfulness anchors you in *what is*.

And this is what so many of us miss—
the fact that life is only ever happening right now.
Not in the past.
Not in the future.
Only here, at this moment.

The past doesn't exist outside your memory.
The future doesn't exist beyond your imagination.
But your body, your child, your breath—they're here. Right now.

When you live in your head, always bracing for what might go wrong or replaying what already has…
you miss the only place life can be lived.
And that's how it all starts to feel like a blur.

That's how we become the mom who says, *"It went by so fast."*

But it doesn't go by fast when you're present.
It goes by *fully*.
Moment by moment, breath by breath.

Presence is the path to clarity.
It's the only place joy lives.
The only place connection happens.
The only place you can truly meet your child—and yourself.

So if you want to feel more calm, more grounded, more like *you*—start by coming back to this breath.
To this sound.
To this moment.

Because right here, right now—
You're not broken.
You're not behind.
You're not failing.

You're just here.
And here is enough.

Science Snapshot

Just 5–7 slow, conscious breaths can lower cortisol and calm your nervous system in under 2 minutes.

This brings your brain out of fight-or-flight and into presence — fast.

Your breath is a built-in reset. Use it anytime, anywhere.

And before you roll your eyes and think, yeah right, I don't have time for this, hear me out.

You don't need an hour of meditation or perfectly quiet space. You just need to shift how you show up in the moments you're already living.

So, the next time you feel stress rising, stop.

Pause for a moment.

Take a really deep breath in through your nose—slow and steady, expand your stomach out.

Hold it for a few seconds.

Then, exhale very slowly through your mouth, as if you're blowing out through a straw.

Feel the tension leaving your body with each breath out.

This simple technique signals your nervous system to calm down, grounding you in the present moment.

That's it.

Ten seconds.

Now, your nervous system gets the message: we're okay, we're safe. There is no panic right now.

And sometimes, that's all it takes to shift the way you feel in the moment.

But for this to truly work, you need to practice this breathing technique correctly. If you don't, you might find yourself thinking, "Breathing never works for me."
The key isn't just taking a breath—it's *how* you take it. When done right, this simple practice can be a powerful reset for your mind and body.

Motherhood is noisy. There's always something demanding your attention. But a few times a day, just pause for a moment and ask yourself:

What am I feeling right now?

That's it. No judgment. No fixing. Just noticing. That tiny pause is enough to shift you out of autopilot.

You don't need a full meditation practice—just choose one daily activity to do with full presence.

- Feel the warmth of your coffee cup.
- Listen to your child's voice as they talk.
- Notice the texture of the laundry in your hands.

These tiny moments anchor you in the now, pulling you out of your head and into your life.

When I started practicing mindfulness, my anxiety didn't magically disappear.
My kids still tested my patience—life was still messy.

But something had shifted: I was no longer consumed by it all.
I could breathe again.
I could hear my kids' laughter, see the joy in their eyes, and actually be in the moment.

So the next time you feel the stress rising, don't reach for perfection—just reach for your breath.

By the way, there's no black belt in mindfulness. No graduation ceremony. There's no final level to master—no finish line to cross. The reward isn't a title.

It's remembering your child's childhood—not just flashes of it.

It's actually *being there* for the little things. The everyday magic. Instead of looking back and realizing you were too distracted to truly see it.

Mindfulness is powerful.
It's not some elusive skill reserved for a select few—it's available to all of us.
You just have to start using it.

But if you want calm to become your natural state—something you can lean on, even in chaos—you have to train for it.

That's what we'll build next.

Step 7—the final step of the MamaZen Method: Train for Calm.

Because while mindfulness can take the edge off—
helping you pause, breathe, and anchor in the moment—
it only opens the door. It brings awareness.

But awareness alone doesn't always shift what's running underneath.
Those deeper patterns—the ones wired into your nervous system—

often need more than presence.
They need rewiring.
They need retraining.

That's when I realized: mindfulness needs a helping hand.
Not to replace it—but to go deeper.
To reach the subconscious mind—the part that stores the fears, habits, triggers, and survival patterns we never chose, but still carry.

That helping hand for me was cognitive hypnotherapy.
It met me where I was, quietly working beneath the surface to release what my conscious mind couldn't touch.
It didn't force calm—it retrained my mind for it.

And that's how MamaZen was born.
From my own need to *feel* different—not just think differently.

The MamaZen Method—and every Mindpower Session inside the app—is built on this miraculous partnership:

Mindfulness to bring you into the now.
Hypnotherapy to rewire what lives beneath it.
One helps you pause.
The other helps you shift.

Together, they create real, lasting change—from the inside out.

Now we're ready to dive into the final step, **Train for Calm**.

MamaZen Moment

Anchor to Now

Reflection:
Take a moment to connect with your body.
Ask yourself:

What is my body feeling right now?

Where do I notice stillness—or tension?

What is happening—right here, right now?

Reframe:
You are not your worries.
You are the calm observer behind them.

Practice:
Three times today, pause and notice something simple:
The feeling of your feet on the ground.
The sound of birds outside.
The color of the sky.

Lisa's Story

Lisa spent years bracing for impact. As a widowed mom with a trauma history, her body lived in survival mode—tense, reactive, always on edge. She had tried therapy, breathing exercises, even meditation, but nothing helped her *feel* different inside.

Mindfulness felt impossible. She couldn't imagine sitting still or clearing her mind—not with grief, responsibility, and noise pressing in from every direction.

Then she found MamaZen. It wasn't about being calm all the time. It was about coming back—again and again—to herself.

"This method didn't make life easy. But it made me present. I learned how to stay with my breath, to soften the edges of my stress, to notice what I was feeling instead of reacting to it."
—*Lisa, MamaZen Member*

Mindfulness didn't erase the hard days.
But it gave her a way to meet them—with clarity, steadiness, and love.
And for the first time in a long time, Lisa wasn't just surviving the day.
She was living in it.

CHAPTER 16

Parenting by Design, Not Default

Before we step into the final phase of the MamaZen Method,

Let's pause.

And take a moment to exhale.

To reflect on the emotional weight you've been carrying…
And begin to release the stories, expectations, and pressure that were never yours to hold.

I used to believe that one day I'd just *arrive*. That I'd wake up and suddenly feel like the mom I was supposed to be—

Calm.
Patient.
Clear.

The kind of mom who always knew what to say, who never lost her cool, who had it all together.

I imagined crossing some invisible finish line and stepping into motherhood with confidence, knowing exactly how to handle every tantrum, every meltdown, every hard conversation. But that day never came. Because parenting isn't a single lesson you master—it's constantly evolving.

Along the way, I've learned that there is no final version of me as a parent.
There's no moment where everything clicks and stays that way. No finish line. No graduation. No point where it suddenly gets easy.

Parenting is a constant process of becoming. Because just as our children are growing, learning, and changing—so are we.

The struggles evolve.
One day it's colic and sleepless nights.
Then tantrums and power struggles.
Then school worries, social drama, and letting go.

And through it all, I've had to learn—again and again—how to come back to myself.
How to breathe through the hard moments.
How to let go of who I thought I should be, and meet myself where I am.

And the same is true for you.
There's no perfect version of you to reach.
Just the version that keeps showing up.
That learns. That adapts. That grows alongside your child.

Every step you've worked through so far?
It wasn't a one-time fix.
It was practice.
A foundation.

These tools—catching yourself, pausing, calming your core, rewriting old patterns—they don't just apply to the hard moments with toddlers or preschoolers.

They're the tools you'll keep coming back to—when the challenges shift, when your kids grow, when life gets louder.

This work evolves with you.

And that's what makes it so powerful.

It doesn't fix every meltdown.

But it gives you something solid to hold on to—when everything else feels like it's constantly changing.

When you recognize the stories that shape your reactions, you gain the power to rewrite them—and lead your parenting with clarity, not conditioning.

It's not about having a perfect plan or the right answer for every moment.

It's about having a set of tools you can return to—patience, mindfulness, self-regulation—especially when things get hard.

Tools that don't just help you *react* better, but help you *feel* better.

Tools that remind you: you're not powerless. You're prepared.

I will never be a perfect parent, because perfection doesn't exist,

But I can be the kind of parent who keeps showing up.

Who keeps learning.

Who trusts that even on the hardest days, I have what I need to keep going.

For so long, I was stuck in reactive mode—always responding to what was happening around me, always feeling like I was one step behind, always bracing for the next meltdown or crisis.

I spent my days putting out fires. One moment, I was calming a crying child; the next, I was refereeing a sibling fight or scrambling to get everyone out the door. I felt like I was constantly catching up, barely staying afloat in the never-ending chaos of motherhood.

And that is how you parent by default instead of by design. I had fallen into patterns which I didn't intentionally choose. My reactions, my tone, the way I handled stress—it was all just happening to me. And worse, most of it was shaped by how I was parented, by the habits and emotional responses I absorbed without even realizing it.

I had never actually stopped to ask myself:

Who do I want to be for my kids?
What kind of energy do I want to bring into our home?

How do I want my kids to remember me?

Because when you don't decide, stress and exhaustion will decide for you.

When you don't choose patience, frustration will take its place. When you don't choose presence, distraction will fill the gap. When you don't choose the type or kind of parent you want to be, you become the parent you never wanted to be.

And I knew exactly what that felt like. The days when I snapped too quickly, when my words were sharper than I intended, when I collapsed at night feeling guilty, promising myself I'd do better tomorrow.

> **Signs You're Parenting by Default (Not Design)**
>
> ▸ Snapping without thinking
> ▸ Feeling like you're always behind
> ▸ Saying things you regret and don't mean
> ▸ Constant guilt or second-guessing
>
> *Default mode isn't your fault. It's what happens when you're running on empty.*

So now, I ask myself daily:

Am I showing up the way I want to?
Do I respond to my kids with love, or am I just reacting out of habit?
Am I creating an environment of calm, connection, and safety?
Do I choose patience, even when it's hard?

Parenting is about the daily decision to show up in a way that aligns with the kind of parent you truly want to be.

And when I look at my kids, when I imagine the mother they'll remember, I don't want them to think of me as the mom who was always overwhelmed, always rushing, always too stressed to enjoy them.

I want them to remember me as the mom who laughed, who listened, who was present. The mom who didn't just react to them but was intentional about how she loved them.

So ask yourself:

What kind of parent do you want to be?

And know this: every single day, you get to decide.

There is a common belief that patience is something you either have or don't have—like a trait you were born with, a fixed part of your personality. Some parents just have that natural, effortless calm, while others have to fight through every moment of frustration.

I thought being a peaceful, present parent was something that just happened to certain people—people who were naturally gentle, who didn't get overwhelmed easily, who somehow always knew how to handle tantrums with a smile.

> **Small Ways to Parent on Purpose**
>
> ▸ One deep breath before responding
>
> ▸ One kind word to yourself in a tough moment
>
> ▸ One tiny act of repair after a hard interaction
>
> ▸ One clear intention in the morning
>
> *One conscious choice can change the energy of an entire day.*

But that's not true.

Patience is a choice.
Presence is a choice.
Calm is a choice.

And those choices aren't made once and for all—they're made in the small moments, every single day.

You make that choice when you pause before you react. When you take one extra breath before you yell. And in the way you choose to show up, even when everything around you feels chaotic.

It's easy to believe that certain emotions just take over—that frustration, impatience, and exhaustion are in control, and we're just along for the ride. But the truth is, we always have a choice.

> *When you pause long enough to choose, you start parenting on purpose.*

It doesn't mean it's easy and that we won't slip up. But the more we practice choosing calm, the more it becomes a part of us.

It's not about perfection.
It's about intention.
It's about showing up on purpose—even when it's hard.

And just by reading this book,
You've already shown that your intention is here.
You're choosing to do the inner work.
You're choosing to show up—on purpose, with love.

It's about recognizing that every challenge is an opportunity to decide:

Do I react the way I always have, or do I try something different?

Do I let stress dictate my response, or do I slow down and choose intention?

Do I let exhaustion define me, or do I give myself the grace to reset and begin again?

Within the mess of parenting, there is also power. The power to choose how we respond. The power to shift our patterns. The power to show up for our kids in a way that aligns with who we truly want to be.

Every small choice you've made so far—catching yourself, pausing, calming your core, rewriting your triggers, setting your energy, choosing your beliefs—has been leading here: the moment you parent from intention, not autopilot.

Now let's move on to the last step in the MamaZen Method:

Step 7 – Train for Calm

Because the kind of parent you want to be doesn't come from trying harder—it comes from training your mind to return to calm, again and again.

MamaZen Moment

Choose Your Anchor

Reflection:
Imagine your child, years from now, describing you to someone.
What three words would you want them to say?
Let those words settle in your heart.

Reframe:
You're not striving to be a perfect parent.
You're becoming a steady anchor they can trust.

Practice:
Each morning this week, ask yourself:

What energy do I want to bring into our home today?

Let that energy lead the way.

Nicole's Story

Nicole used to think patience just wasn't her thing. She'd lose it, then feel awful, and assume she just wasn't built to be one of those calm moms.

But one day, in the middle of yet another tantrum, something felt different. She noticed the tension building—and for once, she didn't snap. It wasn't perfect, but it felt different.

> **"I always thought patience was just something other people had. But I'm learning it's something I can build. Slowly everyday. And that actually gives me hope."**
> —*Nicole, MamaZen Member*

She didn't become calm overnight. But now she knows it's not out of reach—it's something she's practicing, one messy moment at a time.

CHAPTER 17

Mind Training for Moms

Just like you wouldn't expect to run a marathon without training, you can't expect to stay calm under pressure if you don't prepare your mind for it. You need to practice *before* the challenging moments arise—so when they do, your mind is already trained and knows what to do.

Every time you catch yourself, pause, breathe, or choose differently, you're strengthening your mind the same way you'd strengthen a muscle at the gym. Step 7 is about building the endurance to stay calm, even when life (um, parenting) gets messy.

Here's the deal: Your brain is always reinforcing patterns.

If you constantly practice stress, stress will be your default.
If you choose to practice calm, calm will be your default.
If you always react with frustration, frustration will feel automatic.
If you practice being patient, patience will become second nature.

This is why mind practice isn't optional—it's essential. And it's exactly why it's the final step in the MamaZen Method.

It can be anything that helps you:

Shift from reactive to intentional.
Move from overwhelmed to present.
Transition from stressed to calm.

It strengthens your ability to pause, reflect, and make conscious choices—so that instead of defaulting to frustration or guilt, you default to clarity and control.

Some of the best mind practices include:

- **Breathwork**, because it resets your nervous system and helps you stay grounded—especially when emotions run high.

- **Journaling**, because it gives your feelings a place to land, helping you process instead of letting emotions pile up inside.

- **Affirmations**, because they help rewire your subconscious by replacing negative thought loops with empowering truths.

- **Mindpower Sessions by MamaZen**, because they combine all of the above *plus* hypnotherapy. That makes them one of the most powerful tools for retraining the way you think, feel, and respond. In just a few minutes a day, you're strengthening the mental muscle you'll rely on for calm, clarity, and confidence.

Mind Practice = Your Emotional Workout

You don't wait for the pot to boil over—you turn down the heat *before* it spills.
That's what emotional training does.
It helps you stay steady when life turns up the pressure.

And here's the key:
It doesn't matter which practice you choose—what matters is that you choose one. Because if you don't train your mind, it will run on autopilot. And autopilot will take you straight back to stress, reactivity, and guilt.

I practice what I preach. I listen to Mindpower Sessions regularly—not because I have endless time, but because even just 2–5 minutes relaxes my mind and trains it for the chaos.

My emotional state isn't just something that happens to me.
It's something I shape.
Something I train.
Something I strengthen—on purpose.

> **Mind Practice = Your Emotional Workout**
>
> - You can't sprint a mile without training.
> - You can't stay calm in chaos without training either.
> - You wouldn't expect strength without repetition—same goes for emotional control.
> - Every time you pause, breathe, or reset—you're building mental muscle.
>
> *Calm isn't who you are. It's something you build—on purpose.*

Mind practice doesn't have to be long or complicated.

It can also be as simple as:

- A deep breath before reacting.
- A five-minute pause to reset your energy before your kids wake up.
- A short journal entry to process stress instead of letting it spiral in your head.

It doesn't matter how much time you spend training your mind—what matters is that you train it to support you, not sabotage you. Because when you practice calm, patience, and presence daily, they stop feeling like effort.

They start to feel like you.

Imagine this:

It's a chaotic morning.

Your child refuses to put on their shoes.
You're running late.
Your heart starts racing.
You feel the frustration rising, the tension creeping into your body.
Your mind is screaming, "We don't have time for this!"

Before, this would have led to a reaction—

A raised voice.
A snapped command.

That overwhelming sense of why does it always have to be like this?!

Your child would feel it too—your energy, your frustration, your rush.
Maybe they'd fight back. Maybe they'd cry or just completely shut down.

And suddenly, what was once a small moment turns into a power struggle, a stressful start to the day—for both of you.

But now, something shifts.

Instead of reacting, you pause.

You take a deep breath.
You ground yourself in the moment.
You ask yourself one simple, powerful question:

"What kind of parent do I want to be at this moment?"

Do I want to be impatient, rushed, overwhelmed? Or do I want to be calm, patient, present?

That pause—that moment of awareness—helps you shift your reaction.

Not just for you, but for your child.

Your child senses your energy before your words.
When your nervous system is regulated, theirs begins to regulate too.
The storm that was building? It starts to pass.
The moment that could've spiraled? It settles.

When you stay calm:

- **You create safety.** Your child feels grounded—not because you controlled them, but because you controlled yourself.

- **You model emotional regulation.** Your child learns how to manage big feelings by watching you manage yours.

- **You stay connected.** Instead of creating distance with yelling or frustration, you stay emotionally available—even in hard moments.

- **You reduce guilt.** No more replaying the blow-up later and wishing you'd handled it differently. You *did* handle it differently.

- **You build trust.** Your child begins to trust that even when they're struggling, you'll respond with steadiness—not shame.

And that's how calm becomes powerful—not because it controls your child, but because it transforms the space *between* you.

And over time, these choices shape the environment of your home.

Instead of chaos, there's connection.
The power struggles are replaced with understanding.
Guilt turns into peace.

This doesn't mean you'll never lose your patience or that parenting will suddenly be effortless. But it means you'll have a choice.

A choice to be the parent you want to be, not just the one your stress and exhaustion dictate.

Because when we react, we parent from habit. And when we pause, we parent from intention.

Mind Training vs. Willpower

Willpower	Mind Training
Tries to force calm when chaos hits	Builds calm before chaos comes
Relies on luck	Relies on habits
Exhausting	Strengthening

Willpower burns you out. Mind training builds you up.

And isn't that the kind of parent we all want to be?

I don't have all the answers. And I know I never will—because parenting isn't a puzzle to solve or a checklist to complete. My kids will keep growing. Life will keep changing. Some days will stretch me to my edge.

But I'm not empty-handed.

I have my toolbox—and it's powerful.

It's filled with patience that helps me breathe through the chaos.
Mindfulness that brings me back to what really matters.
Self-regulation that stops me from passing my stress onto my kids.
The ability to *pause* before I react—and in that pause, choose better.
And above all, the reminder that I *can choose who I want to be*—again and again.

> **Your calm is a muscle. The more you train it, the more it shows up when you need it most.**

Not perfectly.
But intentionally.

And when I use these tools, parenting feels different.
Not perfect. Not always easy.
But lighter. More connected. More doable.

You've built your foundation. You've learned the steps.
Now it's time to live it—not perfectly, but powerfully.

Because calm parenting isn't just an idea anymore.
It's who you're becoming.

What comes next isn't about learning more.
It's about embodying it—in your home, in your heart, and in the everyday moments that matter most.

MamaZen Moment

The Calm You Build

Reflection:
Think of one chaotic moment you handled better recently.
What did you notice about yourself at that moment?
What new strength emerged?

Reframe:
Calm isn't something you're lucky to have.
It's something you choose—and build—every day.

Practice:
Today, choose just one moment to train:
Pause.
Breathe.
Smile.
This is the work.
And it's working.

Erin's Story

Erin used to snap without thinking. The noise, the mess, the constant demands—it all built up until she exploded. Then came the guilt, and the promise: *Tomorrow, I'll do better.*

One morning, desperate for something to change, she started a two-minute breathing ritual. Just that—two quiet minutes to herself before the chaos.

She didn't expect much. But after a few weeks, something shifted.
The pauses came more naturally. The edge softened. Even under stress, she had a little more space between the trigger and her response.

"I didn't think it would work. But it did. And now I don't start the day without it."
—*Erin, MamaZen Member*

PART 5
Living the Transformation

CHAPTER 18

The Power of Presence

You've started doing the inner work—learning to shift patterns, build awareness, and regulate your emotions.

Now, it's time to settle into what that work makes possible: presence.

Your ability to be truly present—calm, available, attuned—isn't accidental. It's the result of everything you've been building: awareness, regulation, intention, and emotional resilience.

Reaching this point means you've done more than just read about calm parenting—you've started to *live* it. The 7 Steps have guided you through regulating your nervous system, rewiring emotional patterns, shifting your mindset, and approaching parenting with more awareness and intention. Now, the final piece of the parenting puzzle comes together: **presence**.

Presence is more than just being physically there for your child—it's about being emotionally available, grounded, and engaged. It's about showing up in a way that makes your child feel truly seen and heard, fostering a sense of safety and trust that will shape their emotional development for years to come.

When you are truly present, you are not parenting on autopilot, reacting out of stress, frustration, or past conditioning. Instead, you are responding with intention. You are

> *Your child doesn't need you to be perfect. They need you to be present.*

aware of your own emotions and triggers, able to pause before reacting, and capable of guiding your child with calmness and clarity. This presence allows you to enjoy the small, beautiful moments—whether it's the way your child's eyes light up when they tell a story, the sound of their laughter, or the quiet connection of a shared hug.

Being present also strengthens your ability to model emotional regulation, self-compassion, and resilience. Your child learns how to manage their own emotions by watching how you manage yours. They absorb the energy you bring into the home, and when you are present—calm, open, and attuned—they, too, feel secure and at ease.

And presence isn't just a gift for your child—it's a gift for you. When you show up fully in the moment, you shift from feeling overwhelmed by the demands of parenting to experiencing the joy, connection, and deep fulfillment that come with it. You step out of the cycle of guilt and frustration and into a space of appreciation and love.

Mastering the 7 Steps doesn't mean you will be a perfect parent because there is no such thing. It means you will be a conscious one—aware, intentional, and present. And that is what makes all the difference in the world for your child.

Emotional availability is the foundation of a secure parent-child bond and plays a crucial role in shaping a child's emotional development, self-worth, and resilience.

Here is how to be emotionally available to your child:

Be Responsive

Respond to your child with attention and empathy rather than distraction or frustration. When they come to you, whether with a problem, a question, or simply to share a thought, they need to feel that they matter. A distracted or dismissive response can make them feel unimportant, while engaged listening helps them feel valued and understood.

> **Presence Checklist**
>
> You are practicing presence when you:
> - Make real eye contact
> - Offer undivided attention (even briefly)
> - Validate emotions without rushing to fix them
> - Pause before responding
> - Put down your phone when you're with others
>
> *Presence isn't about being perfect. It's about being here.*

Hold Space

Meet their emotions with understanding instead of resistance. When a child is upset, anxious, or overwhelmed, they are not being "difficult"—they are seeking connection and regulation.

Instead of shutting down their feelings or demanding they "calm down," emotional availability means validating their emotions, offering comfort, and helping them navigate their experience.

Be Present

Be in the moment rather than caught up in stress, worry, or your to-do list. It's easy to become consumed by daily tasks and responsibilities, but children thrive on quality of presence, not just quantity of time. Even a few moments of true connection—looking into their eyes, listening without distractions, sharing laughter—can be more impactful than hours spent together while mentally preoccupied.

Be Attuned

When you are emotionally available, your child feels safe, seen, and loved. They learn that their emotions are not a burden but something to be acknowledged and understood. They develop a deep sense of self-worth, knowing that they are valued not just when they are behaving, listening, or meeting expectations, but simply for who they are.

Quick Presence Reset for Busy Moms

- Take 3 slow breaths
- Notice one thing you're grateful for
- Soften your body (drop your shoulders, unclench your jaw)
- Smile (even if you don't feel like it)

One moment of presence can change the emotional climate of your home.

Offer It to Yourself

When you offer that presence to your child, you start to offer it to yourself too. You begin to extend the same patience, understanding, and self-compassion that you show your child. You start to recognize your own emotions without judgment, making space for your needs as well. In this way, emotional availability is not just a gift to your child, it is a transformative shift in how you relate to yourself, your parenting, and your everyday life.

When you bring true presence to your child's hard moments—the tantrums, the fears, the overwhelm—you don't just manage behavior. You teach them how to find their way back to calm too.

And that brings us to what comes next—the power of co-regulation.

MamaZen Moment

The Gift of Being Here

Reflection:
Remember a small moment when you truly felt connected to your child— no distractions, no rushing, just real presence.
How did it feel to simply *be* with them?

Reframe:
Your presence is more powerful than any advice you'll ever give your child.

Practice:

Today, offer your full attention for one small moment:

A 30-second hug.

A shared giggle.

Listening without interrupting.

Let that moment be enough.

Tara's Story

Tara used to spend all day with her daughter—but rarely felt *with* her. Between the dishes, emails, and to-do lists, she was always half-present, half-somewhere else.

One afternoon, she put her phone down, sat on the floor, and gave her daughter five full minutes of undivided attention. No agenda. No distractions. Just presence.

Her daughter's whole body softened. So did Tara's.

"Those five minutes did more for our connection than anything else I'd tried."
—*Tara, MamaZen Member*

She realized it wasn't about doing more—it was about *being there*.

CHAPTER 19

Co-Regulation: Calm Is Contagious

Everything you've been building—the pause, the regulation, the intention—comes to life here. You become the anchor in your child's storm.

Now that you understand the foundational principles of The MamaZen Method, it's time to apply them to everyday parenting challenges. This section is where the real transformation happens, where mindfulness, intention, and calm meet the unpredictable, messy realities of parenting.

No matter how much inner work we do, there will be tantrums, meltdowns, moments of exhaustion, and days where patience feels impossible. But instead of reacting in frustration or feeling defeated, you have the tools to navigate these challenges with confidence, emotional resilience, and self-compassion.

There's a moment every parent dreads. The screaming, the tears, the defiance. Maybe it's happening in the grocery store, in the middle of bedtime, or right as you're trying to get out the door. Your child is completely overwhelmed by their emotions, and you feel like you're on the verge of losing it too.

You take a deep breath, trying to keep your own frustration in check. But deep down, you just want it to stop. You want them to calm down, listen, cooperate, anything but this meltdown.

I get it. I've been there more times than I can count. And if you're anything like me, you've probably found yourself reacting in ways you later regret. Maybe you've snapped, yelled, or sent them to their room just to make the chaos stop.

But here's the painful truth: our children's emotions are not the problem. Our own emotional state in those moments is what determines whether the situation escalates or calms down.

When you're grounded, you can guide your child through their emotions. When you're dysregulated, you're more likely to meet their storm with a storm of your own.

This chapter is about breaking that cycle, not through force or punishment, but through co-regulation. Instead of controlling your child's emotions, you'll learn how to guide them through their big feelings with connection, patience, and emotional intelligence.

For a long time, parenting was built around control. The idea was that if children misbehave, they needed to be corrected, punished, or isolated until they "got it together."

But emotions don't work that way.

Think about the last time you were overwhelmed, frustrated, or sad. Did someone telling you to "calm down" make you feel better? Probably not.

Children don't calm down because they are told to. They calm down because they feel safe enough to regulate.

That's where co-regulation comes in.

Co-regulation is the process of helping your child manage their emotions by being a steady, calming presence instead of trying to control them. It's about teaching regulation by showing them what it looks like.

When Control Makes Things Worse

- "Stop crying!" → child feels ashamed and unsafe
- "Go to your room!" → child feels isolated and misunderstood
- "Calm down now!" → child's body feels attacked and escalates more

Trying to control the behavior often disconnects us from the emotion underneath.

Think of it like this: when your child is having a meltdown, they are a storm. Their emotions are swirling, unpredictable, and intense. If you try to stop the storm by yelling, threatening, or controlling, it only grows stronger.

But if you remain steady, calm, grounded, and present, you become the anchor. And over time, they learn to steady themselves too.

Let's take a moment to explore the difference between control-based parenting and co-regulation. Many of us were raised with the idea that a child's emotions should be managed through discipline, consequences, or shutting them down as quickly as possible. But when we approach emotional moments from a place of control, we unintentionally send the message that big feelings are unacceptable, inconvenient, or something to be suppressed.

Co-regulation, on the other hand, shifts the focus from stopping emotions to guiding children through them. Instead of seeing meltdowns, defiance, or frustration as behaviors to be fixed, we recognize them as opportunities to model emotional regulation. By staying present, offering support, and helping children understand their emotions, we teach them how to navigate challenges in a healthy way.

Let's take a look at a few examples of how control-based reactions differ from co-regulation:

Control (Reaction-Based)	Co-Regulation (Connection-Based)
"Stop crying right now!"	"I see you're really upset. I'm here."
"Go to your room until you calm down!"	"Let's take a moment to breathe together."
"If you keep this up, you're losing your toy!"	"I see you're frustrated. Let's figure this out together."

Control focuses on stopping emotions. Co-regulation focuses on guiding them.

Your child's meltdown is not your emergency. Their emotions are not a reflection of your parenting. Your job at the moment is not to control them but to be the steady presence they need in order to work through their emotions.

Here's how you can stay calm when your child is overwhelmed:

1. Before responding, take one deep breath in through your nose, hold for a moment, and exhale slowly through your mouth. This signals your nervous system that you are safe, which allows you to respond from a regulated place rather than reacting from frustration. Even one breath can help you shift from reactive to intentional.

2. Next, remind Yourself: "This is Not an Emergency". When your child is in distress, your brain might interpret it as a crisis, triggering fight-or-flight mode. But meltdowns, defiance, and big emotions are not true emergencies, they are opportunities for connection.

3. Silently tell yourself:
   I am safe. My child is safe.
   They are having a hard time, not giving me a hard time.
   This simple step of reframing their behavior helps you shift from anger or frustration to empathy and presence.

4. Next, get low and make eye contact. When your child is overwhelmed, they may feel lost in their emotions. Instead of towering over them, get down to their level. This simple act can help them feel less alone and more supported. Lower

your voice instead of raising it. A calm tone helps regulate their nervous system. Soft eye contact shows them that you are present and not upset with them. Your body language speaks louder than words—when you appear calm and open, they will begin to mirror your energy.

5. Yes, it is important to validate their feelings. Instead of jumping to problem-solving or discipline, first acknowledge what they are feeling. When children feel seen and understood, they are more likely to move through their emotions faster.

    Try saying:
    "I see that you're really upset right now."
    "It's okay to feel frustrated. I'm here."
    "I know this is hard for you."

    You're not agreeing with their behavior—you're simply letting them know it's okay to have big feelings.

6. You can offer a comforting touch (if they accept it). For some kids, gentle physical touch can help them feel safe and regulated. A hand on their back, a hug, or even holding their hand can signal to their nervous system that they are supported.

    If they pull away, respect that boundary. Some kids need space to process before they can reconnect.

7. Speak less and breathe more. Your breathing is contagious. I've noticed it firsthand with my kids; when their emotions

are running high, my instinct used to be to tell them to calm down, to stop crying, or to fix it for them. But now, I simply breathe. I slow down and take steady breaths, and tell them to match my breath. Their frantic gasps start syncing with mine. Their bodies soften. Their nervous systems catch the rhythm of my calm. When emotions are high, your child's brain is in fight-or-flight mode. They are not in a place to process long explanations or logic. Instead of trying to reason with them, focus on being calm and present.

8. Try using these minimal, calming phrases:
   "I'm here with you."
   "We'll figure this out together."
   "Let's take a breath together."

   This moment is less about talking and more about being.

9. Offer them a choice but without pressure; this will give your child a sense of control without demanding obedience.

   Instead of saying: *"Calm down right now!"*
   Try saying: *"Would you like to take a breath with me or squeeze this pillow?"*

   Instead of saying: *"Stop screaming!"*
   Tell them: *"You're really upset. Do you want to sit with me or take a break in your cozy spot?"*

10. Or use a calming activity, like:
    "Let's breathe in like we're smelling a flower and out like we're

blowing out a candle."

"Tell me 5 things you see, 4 things you can touch, 3 things you hear, 2 things you smell, and 1 thing you taste."

"Would you like to hold your stuffed animal while we talk?"
These sensory-based techniques help reset your child's nervous system.

11. Give them time, you can't rush a child out of their emotions. If they are still overwhelmed, give them the time they need. Let them cry. Let them express themselves. Stay close, but don't force them to calm down on your timeline.

    Once they start to settle, that's when you can guide them through a solution.

12. And last, once they are regulated, that's the time to help them learn from the experience. Talk about what happened in a calm, non-judgmental way—without shame, blame, or urgency. This is when their brain is open to reflection, not when they're still in the middle of big emotions.

From my experience, every time I approach my child with curiosity rather than criticism, they naturally acknowledge their reaction. They recognize, in their own words, that they overreacted and express a desire to handle it differently next time. It's not forced; it's not something I have to make them say. It comes from them—because deep down, they don't enjoy feeling out of control either.

They don't want to be stuck in those moments any more than we do.

When we approach these conversations with patience and connection, we create a space where they can develop self-awareness, where they learn to regulate, reflect, and grow, rather than feel ashamed or defensive.

Here are some key questions you can ask after the moment has passed:

> **Co-Regulation Cheat Sheet**
>
> ▶ Get on their level (physically)
> ▶ Breathe slower, not faster
> ▶ Speak less, soften your voice
> ▶ Validate first: *"It's okay to be upset."*
> ▶ Offer safety, not shame
>
> *Your calm body teaches theirs how to settle.*

"What was really hard for you at that moment?"
"What do you think might help next time?"
"Would you like to come up with a plan together for when this happens again?"

The long-term impact of co-regulation is powerful. It shapes your child's ability to manage emotions, build resilience, and feel deeply secure. When co-regulation happens consistently, kids learn that emotions aren't scary or something to push down—they're signals to notice, understand, and move through.

Over time, this strengthens their ability to self-regulate, helping them navigate frustration, disappointment, and stress with greater ease. It also fosters a strong foundation of trust and connection between you and your child, which helps reduce the need for power struggles, yelling, or punitive discipline.

Instead of feeling alone in their emotions, children who experience co-regulation learn that feelings are manageable, that they are safe in expressing them, and that they have the inner tools to process challenges in a healthy way.

By choosing co-regulation over control, you're not just getting through a meltdown. You're raising a child who can handle life—with calm, with confidence, with compassion.

> **When your child is overwhelmed, your calm is the most powerful tool in the room.**

Every meltdown you meet with calm…
Every tough moment you stay steady…
You're not just parenting—you're shaping your child's emotional future.
Calm isn't something you hope for anymore. It's something you choose.

MamaZen Moment

Anchor in the Storm

Reflection:
Think about the last time your child had a big emotion.
What did *you* need at that moment?
What would have helped you stay grounded?

Reframe:
My child isn't giving me a hard time.
They're having a hard time.
And I have the power to help them through it—
with my calm.

Practice:
When emotions rise today—yours or your child's—
take one long, slow breath.
Place your hand over your heart and think:
I am the anchor, not the storm.

Jillian's Story

After giving birth to her second baby, Jillian found herself stuck in a cycle of anger, overwhelm, and guilt. Her toddler started reflecting that anger back—tantrums, yelling, big emotions that felt all too familiar.

"She's picking up on my anger," Jillian realized. **"And it's coming out in her."**

That moment was her wake-up call.

Jillian began listening to MamaZen sessions—and her daughter started joining in too.

"She just lies there with her eyes closed, smiling," Jillian said. *"Like she's soaking it in."*
—Jillian, MamaZen App Member

Jillian stopped trying to shut the tantrums down. Instead, she started anchoring herself first.

"Healing starts from the inside," she said. And once she began calming her own body, something shifted in her daughter too.

Because calm isn't something we force on our kids. It's something we model—one breath, one moment, at a time.

CHAPTER 20

Choosing Harmony Every Day

"Your kids are so calm."

"They're confident, happy. They just seem to know what to expect."

I hear these comments from other moms all the time. I don't say this from a place of arrogance, but because I have done and continue to do the work so they can thrive.

Sometimes, I think about the other way it could have gone, and my whole body tenses. We all come into this journey unprepared, unaware, and already feeling behind. But something inside me refused to accept that as my reality.

I wanted my dream of parenthood to be real. Not the perfect version from movies, because that doesn't exist, but a version where my children feel safe, loved, and secure. Where every day ends with a smile, and every morning starts with a hug.

And I know now that calm isn't something you wait for, it's something you create.

I communicate. I pause. I think before I react. I parent with intention.

Will things go wrong? Of course. Will I feel like I'm failing at times? Probably. But those thoughts will pass, like the wind. And no matter what, I will always return to my inner peace, knowing that I have done the work.

The fact that you are here, reading these words, means that something inside you has already begun to transform. You are more aware, more mindful, more intentional than you were before. That is progress. Change isn't about flipping a switch, it's about the small moments, the everyday choices that shape your reality. Every time you pause instead of react, every time you choose connection over control, you are doing the work. And that work will continue to build, one mindful choice at a time. This is how transformation happens, not in a single moment, but in the accumulation of many small, quiet victories.

Motherhood can feel lonely, even when you're surrounded by people. It's easy to believe that you're the only one struggling, that other moms have it all figured out. But, behind closed doors, every mother has felt lost. Every mother has questioned herself. Every mother has had nights where she lays awake, wondering if she's doing enough. You are not failing. You are not broken. And most importantly, you are not alone. Billions of mothers have walked this path before you, and millions more are walking it beside you now. If you feel overwhelmed, remind yourself that you are part of something bigger, a community of mothers all trying their best, just like you.

Your words matter, but your actions matter more. The way you handle stress, the way you treat yourself, the way you navigate difficult moments—your child is watching and learning from it all. They see when you take a deep breath instead of snapping. They notice when you apologize, when you show kindness, when you regulate your emotions instead of letting them control you. This is how they learn. They learn self-compassion by seeing you forgive yourself. They learn resilience by watching you get back up after hard days. They learn emotional regulation because you are modeling it for them. You don't have to be perfect, your job is to show them how to be human. And by doing the work on yourself, you are giving them a gift that will last a lifetime.

You Are the Calm at the Center

Not the messy floors.
Not the undone lists.
Not the loud moments nor the quiet tears.

But the love in your presence.
The steadiness in your return.
The safety in your arms.

This is what creates home.

There will be days when it feels like all the progress you've made disappears in an instant. When the stress piles up, when exhaustion takes over, when you slip back into old patterns. That doesn't mean you've failed. It means you're human. Growth isn't a straight line, it's a lifelong process of learning, unlearning, and relearning. The goal is not to never lose your patience or to never struggle again. The goal is to always know how to find your way back. You will get off track, but you will also return, again and again. That's what matters. So give yourself grace. Extend to yourself the same patience and understanding you give your children. You are doing the best you can, and that is enough.

Now that you've come to the end of this book, what's next? The real work begins now—integrating what you've learned into your daily life. Maybe that means starting your mornings with an intention, or listening to a Mindpower Session when you feel overwhelmed. Maybe it means catching yourself in the moment before reacting and choosing to respond differently. Whatever it is, remember that you have everything you need. You don't have to have it all figured out today, just take it one moment, one breath, one choice at a time. And when you need support, you know where to find it.

You will still have hard days. Your children will test your patience. Life will throw unexpected challenges your way. But through it all, you will know the path back to yourself.

You will know how to shift.
You will know how to breathe.
You will know how to parent with mindfulness, intention, and calm.

Because when you show up as that parent, you're not just helping your child thrive—you're giving them the inner tools to face an unpredictable world with strength and grace. This is how generational cycles break—one conscious choice, one calm response, one moment at a time. Now, you get to rewrite the story— not just for you and your children, but for their children, and generations beyond.

> *Peace in motherhood doesn't come from getting it all right— but from choosing to return to love, again and again.*

That is the power you hold.

MamaZen Moment

I Am the Calm

Reflection:
Right now, place a hand over your heart.
Feel your breath move in ... and out.
Connect to the part of you that knows:
You are the calm your child will one day remember.

Reframe:
I'm not chasing calm.
I'm creating it—breath by breath.

> **Practice:**
>
> Tonight, before you sleep, whisper to yourself:
>
> *I am always enough.*
>
> *I am always becoming.*

Lauren's Story

Lauren is a mother of six, with kids ranging from 6 to 19. She's a full-time teacher, homeschooling four of her children, and pursuing her master's degree. Her days were a blur—lesson plans, household demands, emotional labor. Like so many mothers, she was pouring everything she had into everyone else.

By the end of the day, she felt completely depleted.

She had tried yoga and meditation before, hoping to find relief. But nothing stuck.
"It all felt hokey," she said. **"Or like it just didn't work."**

Then, one night before bed, she tried a sleep session on MamaZen. Not as part of some perfect routine—just ten quiet minutes for herself.

"It helped me sleep. My body relaxed. And I didn't wake up feeling tight and anxious the way I usually do."
—*Lauren, MamaZen Member*

In those ten minutes, she stopped abandoning herself. Her breath deepened. Her thoughts slowed. And when she woke up the next morning, she felt a little more present—with her kids, and with herself.

For the first time in years, she wasn't doing it to become a better mom.
She was doing it because *she mattered, too.*

Reference Guide

The MamaZen Method: 7 Steps Quick Reference Guide

Step 1: Catch Yourself
Notice when you're stuck in old patterns instead of judging yourself.
You can't change what you don't see.

Step 2: Hit Pause
Interrupt the autopilot reactions. Even one deep breath can rewrite the moment.
Space creates choice.

Step 3: Calm Your Core
Reset your body before your emotions take over.
You can't parent calmly when your body thinks it's in danger.

Step 4: Heal from Your Past
Release old pain so you don't parent from it.
You can't move forward when the past is still driving.

Step 5: Choose Your Energy
Decide how you want to feel — before life chooses for you.
Lead your day, don't chase it.

Step 6: Parent on Purpose
When you change your inner script, you change how you show up.
Stop reacting out of habit. Start leading from who you want to be.

Step 7: Train for Calm
Strengthen your emotional muscles every day — before you need them.
Calm isn't luck. It's training.

Turn The MamaZen Method Into a Way of Being

You've just learned the 7 Steps of the MamaZen Method.

If you'd like to bring them into your everyday life—not just as concepts, but as daily moments of calm, clarity, and connection, the MamaZen app was created to guide you through that journey.

Whether you're feeling overwhelmed, stuck in old patterns, or simply need a few minutes to breathe, the app is there to support you in real time, 24/7.

Inside, you'll find for both you and your kids:

- Guided Mindpower Sessions® that align with each of the 7 Steps
- Tools to calm your nervous system and shift your emotional state
- Gentle support to help you parent with more intention, presence, and peace

This is how change becomes lasting.
This is how the method becomes your way of being.

To download the app, search "MamaZen" in the App Store or Google Play, **or scan the QR code below to unlock 30 days free—just for readers of this book.**

www.ingramcontent.com/pod-product-compliance
Lightning Source LLC
Chambersburg PA
CBHW050519100526
44581CB00001B/32